W9-AYI-417

my Book 2

Authors and Advisors

Alma Flor Ada • Kylene Beers • F. Isabel Campoy

Joyce Armstrong Carroll • Nathan Clemens

Anne Cunningham • Martha C. Hougen

Elena Izquierdo • Carol Jago • Erik Palmer

Robert E. Probst • Shane Templeton • Julie Washington

Contributing Consultants

David Dockterman • Mindset Works®

Jill Eggleton

Printed in the U.S.A.

ISBN   978-1-328-51697-8

5 6 7 8 9 10   0868   27 26 25 24 23 22 21 20

4500800011   C D E F G

HMH

into Reading™

my Book 2

Welcome to myBook!

Do you like to read different kinds of texts for all kinds of reasons? Do you have a favorite genre or author? What can you learn from a video? Do you think carefully about what you read and view?

Here are some tips to get the MOST out of what you read and view:

Set a Purpose. What is the title? What is the genre? What do you want to learn from this text or video? What about it looks interesting to you?

Read and Annotate. As you read, underline and highlight important words and ideas. Make notes about things you want to figure out or remember. What questions do you have? What are your favorite parts? Write them down!

Make Connections. How does the text or video connect to what you already know? To other texts or videos? To your own life or community? Talk to others about your ideas. Listen to their ideas, too.

Wrap It Up! Look back at your questions and annotations. What did you like best? What did you learn? What do you still want to know? How will you find out?

As you read the texts and watch the videos in this book, make sure you get the MOST out of them by using the tips above.

But, don't stop there . . . Decide what makes you curious, find out more about it, have fun, and never stop learning!

MODULE 7

Make a Difference

MODULE 10

Tell a Tale

MODULE 6

Animal Behaviors

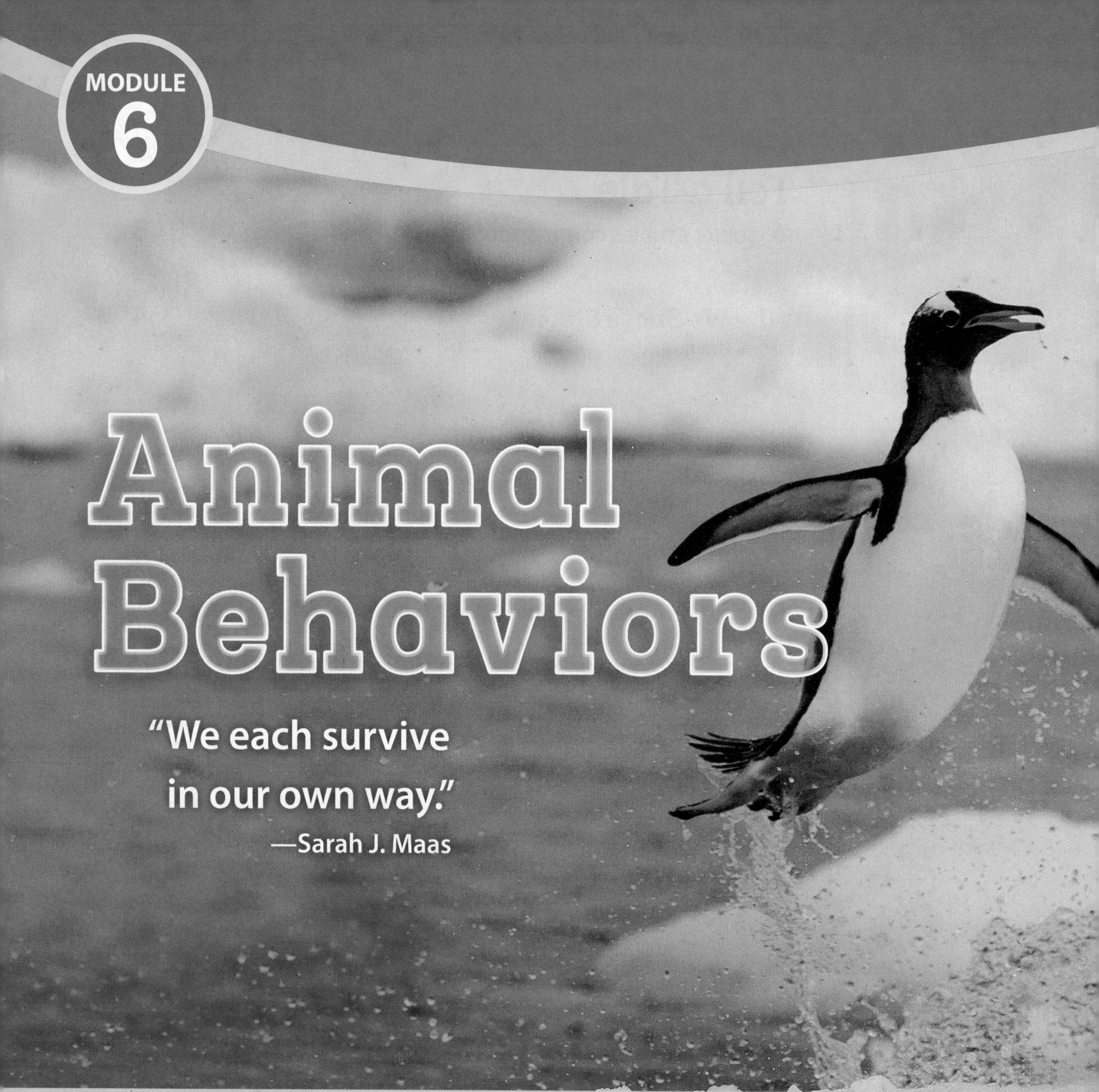

"We each survive in our own way."
—Sarah J. Maas

? Essential Question

What behaviors help animals survive?

Get Curious
Video

Words About Animal Behaviors

The words in the chart below will help you talk and write about the texts in this module. Which words about animal behaviors have you seen before? Which words are new to you?

Add to the Vocabulary Network on page 13 by writing synonyms, antonyms, and related words and phrases for each word.

After you read each selection in this module, come back to the Vocabulary Network and keep building it. Add more ovals if you need to.

WORD	MEANING	CONTEXT SENTENCE
hatch (verb)	An animal will hatch from an egg when it breaks out of the shell by itself.	We were amazed when we saw the turtle hatch from its egg.
universal (adjective)	When something is universal, it applies to everyone.	All living things have a universal need for water.
span (noun)	A span is a period of time between two events or dates, usually marking something important.	Bulldogs have a life span of about 8 to 10 years.
growth (noun)	Growth happens when someone or something gets older and/or bigger.	The scientist measured the growth of the baby turtle.

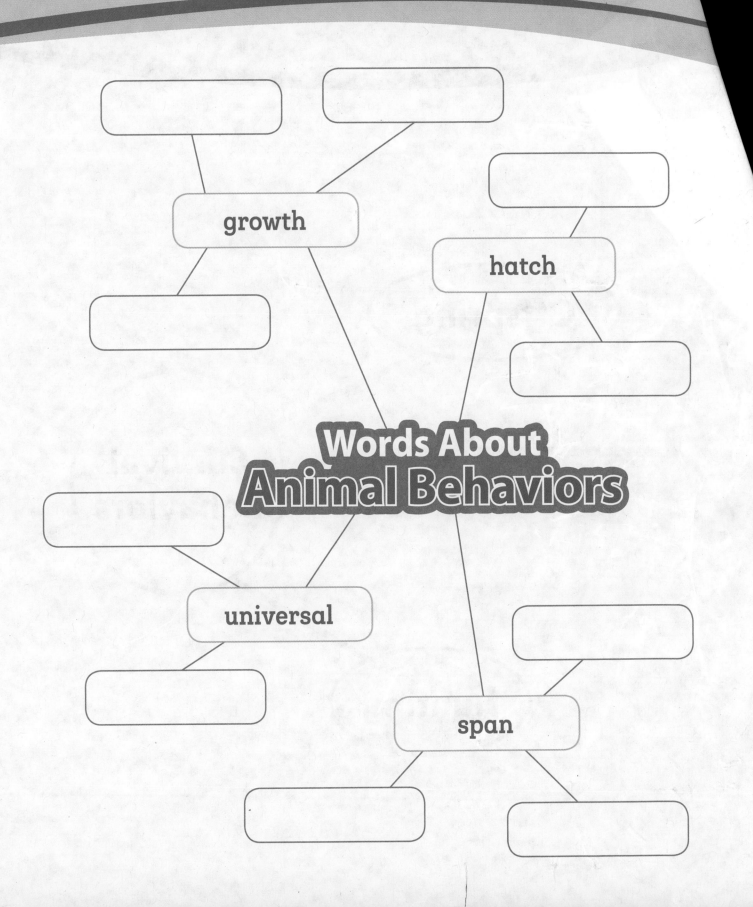

growth

hatch

Words About
Animal Behaviors

universal

span

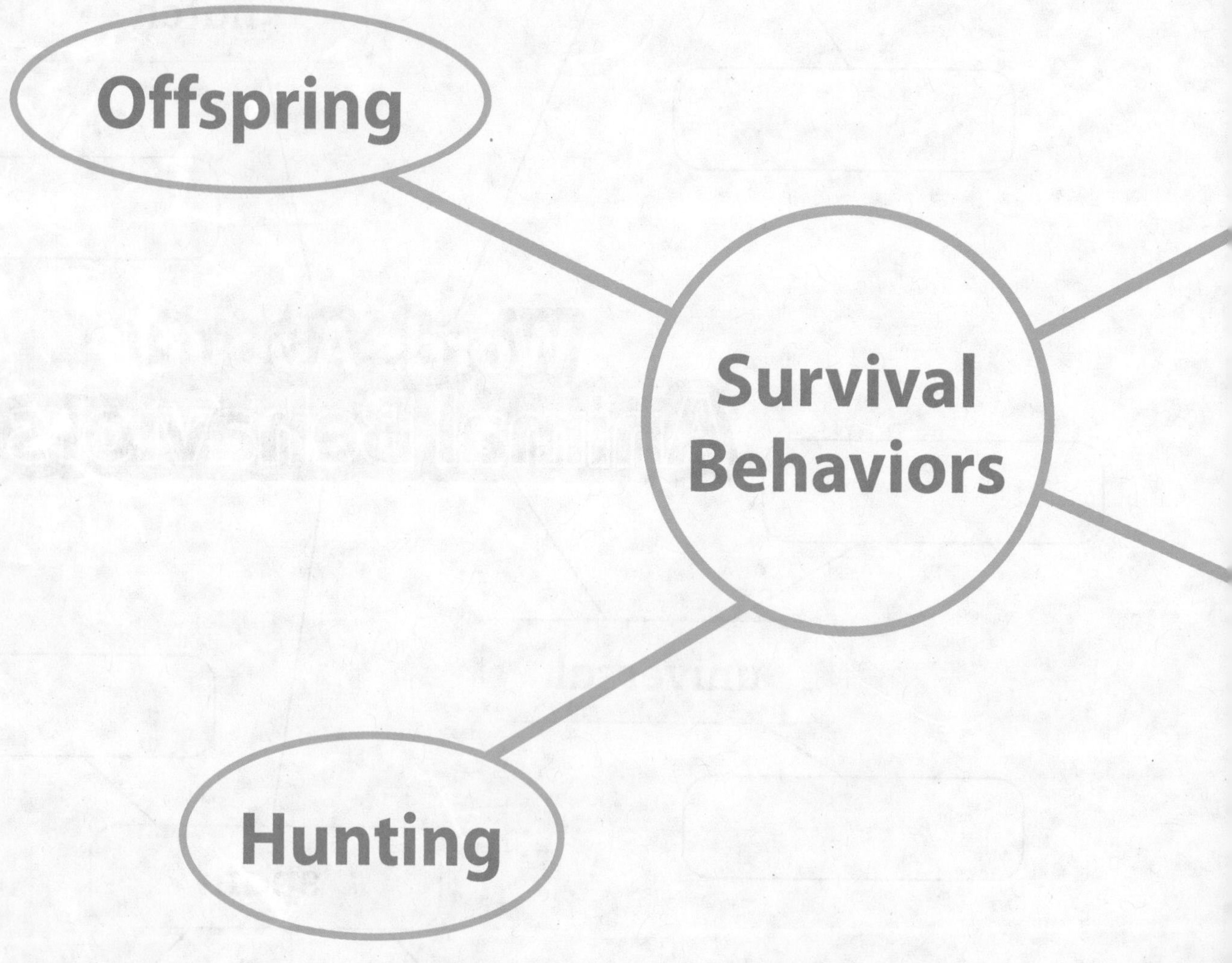

Offspring

Survival Behaviors

Hunting

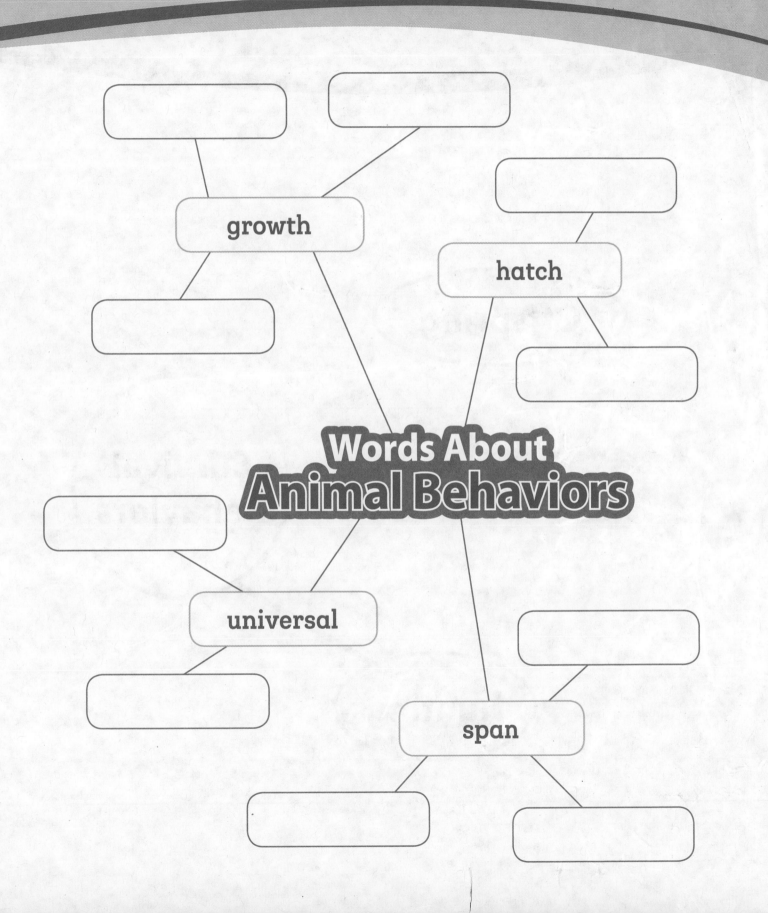

Words About Animal Behaviors

growth

hatch

universal

span

13

Knowledge Map

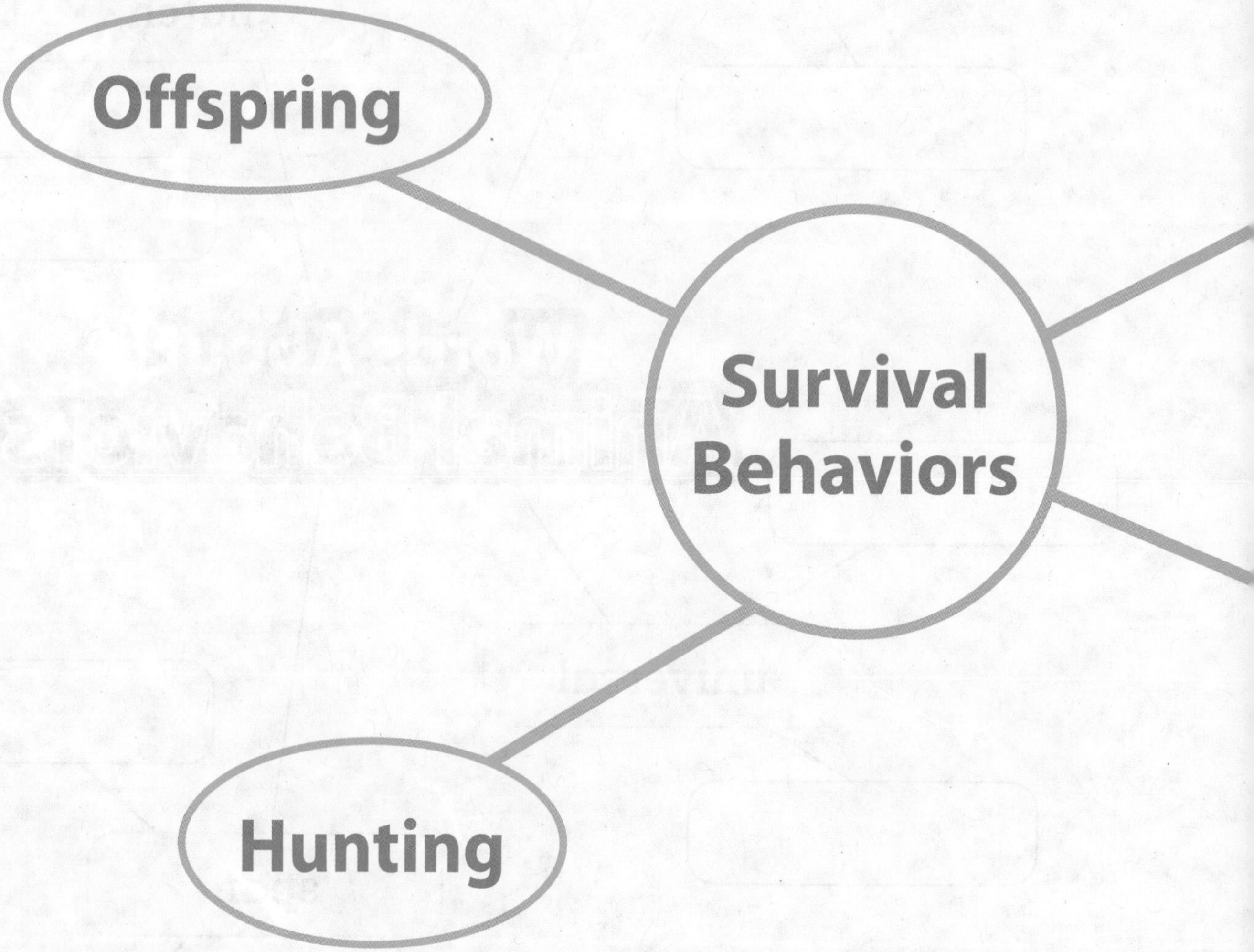
Offspring
Survival Behaviors
Hunting

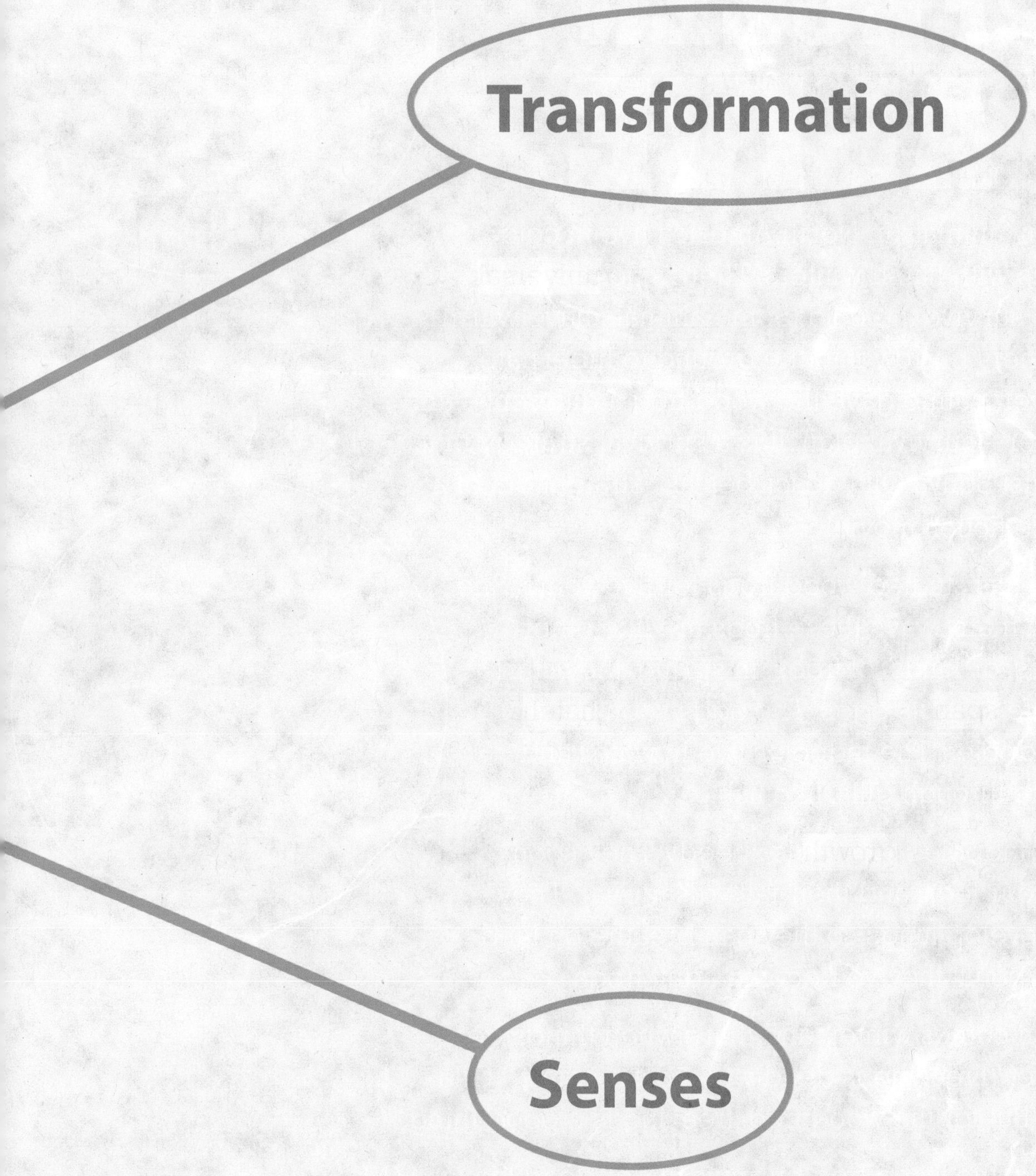

Transformation

Senses

FROZEN ALIVE

4. When cold temperatures come, the frog burrows under leaves.

1   Many animals in North America live in cold regions with harsh winters. There's no universal way to survive the cold. Some animals have warm fur. Others burrow into the ground to hibernate. However, nature gave the wood frog a different—and stranger—survival plan. It is a survival strategy that biologist Sonya Olla describes as "straight out of a science fiction movie!"

2   Olla has studied wood frogs for five years. She says in many ways these frogs are like other species, or kinds, of frogs. In spring, they start their life span as eggs. The eggs soon hatch into tadpoles. The tadpoles live in water and breathe through gills, like fish.

3   The tadpole's growth is speedy. They soon grow four legs, and their tails disappear. They also develop lungs so they can breathe on land. At this point, they've become adult frogs.

3. The tadpole forms legs and loses its tail. It is now an adult frog.

4   Then comes winter, and that's when things get strange. "Freezing is deadly to most animals," Olla says. "But for the wood frog, freezing is a *good* thing."

5   "First, the wood frog burrows under dead leaves," Olla explains. "However, this doesn't protect it from the cold. Something interesting happens in the frog's cells."

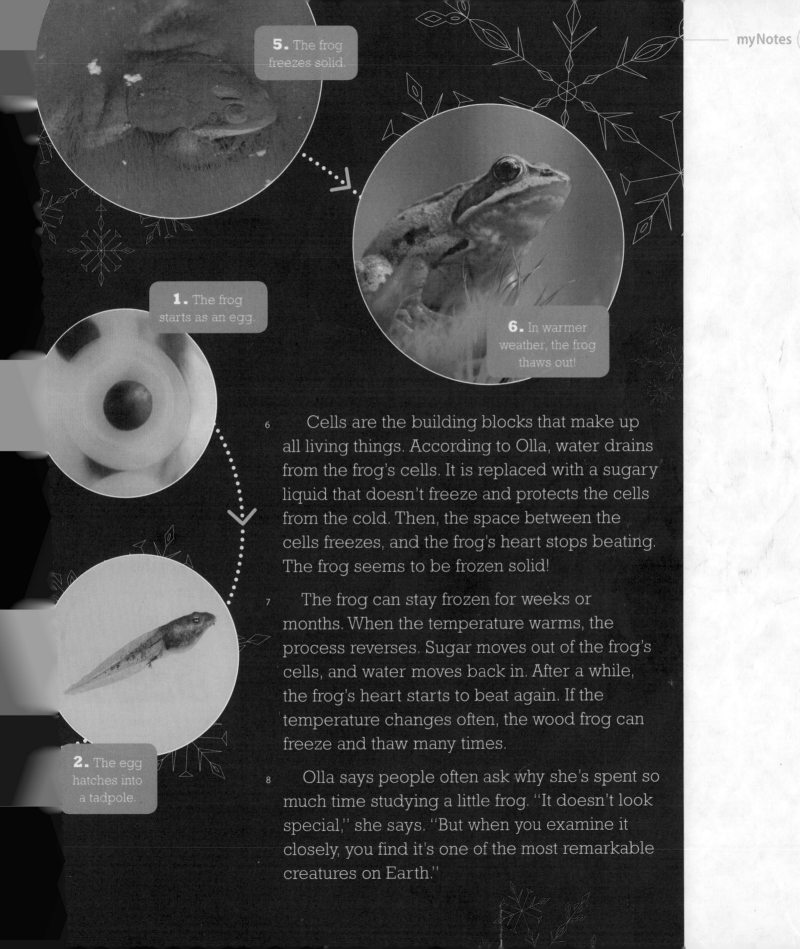

5. The frog freezes solid.

1. The frog starts as an egg.

6. In warmer weather, the frog thaws out!

2. The egg hatches into a tadpole.

6   Cells are the building blocks that make up all living things. According to Olla, water drains from the frog's cells. It is replaced with a sugary liquid that doesn't freeze and protects the cells from the cold. Then, the space between the cells freezes, and the frog's heart stops beating. The frog seems to be frozen solid!

7   The frog can stay frozen for weeks or months. When the temperature warms, the process reverses. Sugar moves out of the frog's cells, and water moves back in. After a while, the frog's heart starts to beat again. If the temperature changes often, the wood frog can freeze and thaw many times.

8   Olla says people often ask why she's spent so much time studying a little frog. "It doesn't look special," she says. "But when you examine it closely, you find it's one of the most remarkable creatures on Earth."

Prepare to Read

GENRE STUDY This text is a multi-genre text. It is both a **narrative nonfiction** and a **fantasy**. **Narrative nonfiction** gives factual information. A **fantasy** is an unrealistic fiction story.

- Authors of narrative nonfiction texts may organize their ideas around a central, or main, idea.
- Narrative nonfiction includes visuals, such as photographs, illustrations, maps, and diagrams.
- Fantasies are unrealistic. They include talking animals or characters and objects with special powers.

SET A PURPOSE **Think about** the title and genre of this text. This text is about a dragonfly. What do you know about dragonflies? What would you like to learn? Write your responses below.

Meet the Author and Illustrator:
Heather Lynn Miller and
Michael Chesworth

CRITICAL VOCABULARY

larvae

molt

unsuspecting

deposited

patch

cumbersome

THIS IS YOUR LIFE CYCLE

with special guest
Dahlia the dragonfly

Written by *Heather Lynn Miller*   Illustrated by *Michael Chesworth*

1 *Good evening, larvae, nymphs, and insects! This is Bob Beetle, welcoming you to another episode of* **THIS IS YOUR LIFE CYCLE** *The show that follows the life cycle of everybody's favorite class of animals, the insects!*

2 *Each week we take our cameras to the hot spots of the bug world to follow insects as they begin their lives as eggs, hatch as nymphs or larvae, and molt into fully developed adults.*

larvae   Insects that have just hatched and haven't yet changed to their adult form are called larvae.

molt   When insects or other animals molt, they lose their outer covering, such as skin or feathers.

3   *Tonight we're coming to you live from a swamp, hidden by darkness, under the branch of a weeping willow. It may look peaceful from here, but beneath the surface of the water, our special guest, Dahlia, has spent the past two years fighting for her life.*

4   That's right, folks—Dahlia has slipped through the jaws of
hungry predators like:

5   Breathe easy, my friends. Dahlia is one tough little nymph and has
managed to escape death by living under the cover of rotting leaves,
dead logs, and thick swamp grasses.

6 *Word from the pond says she's become quite a fierce little predator herself. Why, just last week,* The Daily Buzz *reported seeing Dahlia chomp away at an unsuspecting tadpole.*

unsuspecting   If you are unsuspecting, you do not notice something that is happening or may happen.

23

7 *Ladies and gentlemen, I've just been told that Fly Guy is standing by with exciting news. Guy, what do you see?*

8 Bob, I'm doing a flyby of the water's surface now. I get the strong sense that something amazing is about to happen . . .

9 Hold on, the water is beginning to ripple! I think Dahlia may be ready to emerge.

10 I'm going to try to land on a nearby twig for a closer look.

11   *Can you see anything, Guy?*

12   Bob, I see something! She's pulling herself out of the water with her strong front legs. We should see her head any moment now.

13   *Remember, audience—we need complete silence. We don't want to frighten Dahlia.*

     Shhhhhhhhhh . . .

25

17 *You're just in time to hear a message*
from our first mystery guest.
Dahlia, do you remember this voice?

18 I'm so glad you made it to the surface without being eaten by some nasty bass. I remember the day I deposited you and your brothers and sisters. You were all such sweet, tiny eggs.

19 Mom, is that you?

Mystery Guest #1

deposited If you deposited something in a place, you left it there.

27

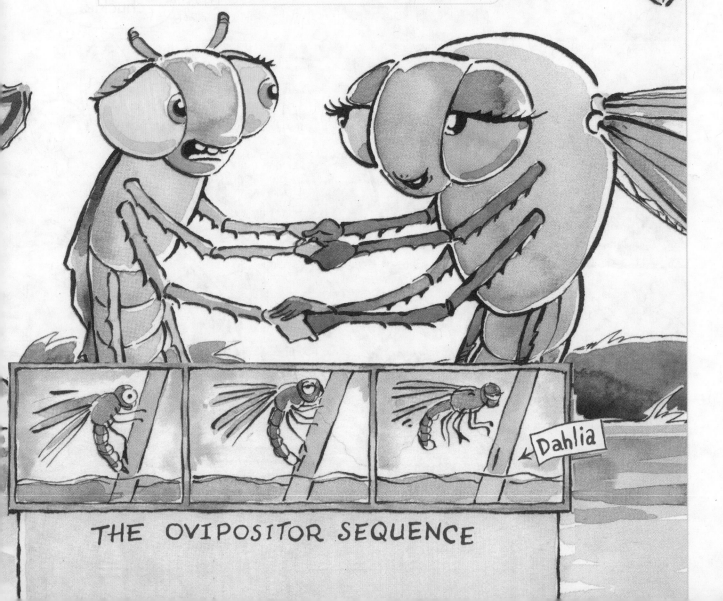

21 I found a perfect patch of swamp grass with tall, tender shoots. It was such a beautiful spot. I whipped out my ovipositor and went to work poking tiny holes in the blades of grass. I knew that laying my eggs inside would help keep you safe from hungry fish. By the end of the day, I had laid over 800 eggs. I was so exhausted when I finished, I just sat down and died.

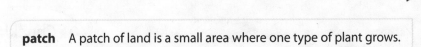

patch A patch of land is a small area where one type of plant grows.

THE OVIPOSITOR SEQUENCE

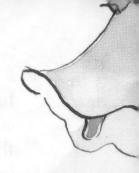

22 *We all know how that goes—right, audience? It's the story of an insect's life. We hatch, we grow, we mate, we die!*

23 *Dahlia, you stayed tucked inside that blade of swamp grass for several weeks. Then one day, your egg casing split, and you—*

24 Chuckle, chuckle.

a white wiggling nymph—slipped into the open water of the pond.

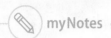

25 *And that's where our next mystery guest found you.*

26 When I saw you, Dahlia, you looked so tasty. I was young, taking my first dive out of the nest, and I was starving. You would have made a perfect snack.

27 I know this one, Bob. I'll never forget Box Turtle, the most frightening beast I've ever met. He slid down from a lily pad and tried to eat me alive!

Mystery Guest #2

28 *Poor Dahlia. What did you do?*

29 The only thing I knew how to do—wiggle!

30 You wiggled, all right. You wiggled your rear end into the muck at the bottom of the pond. Before I had a chance to gobble you up, you disappeared under a pile of dead leaves.

31 *On the day you became a nymph, Dahlia, you also became a hungry predator. And you found a new way to travel. Your water jet system helped you zip through the water at rocket speed. Can you tell us how it worked?*

34

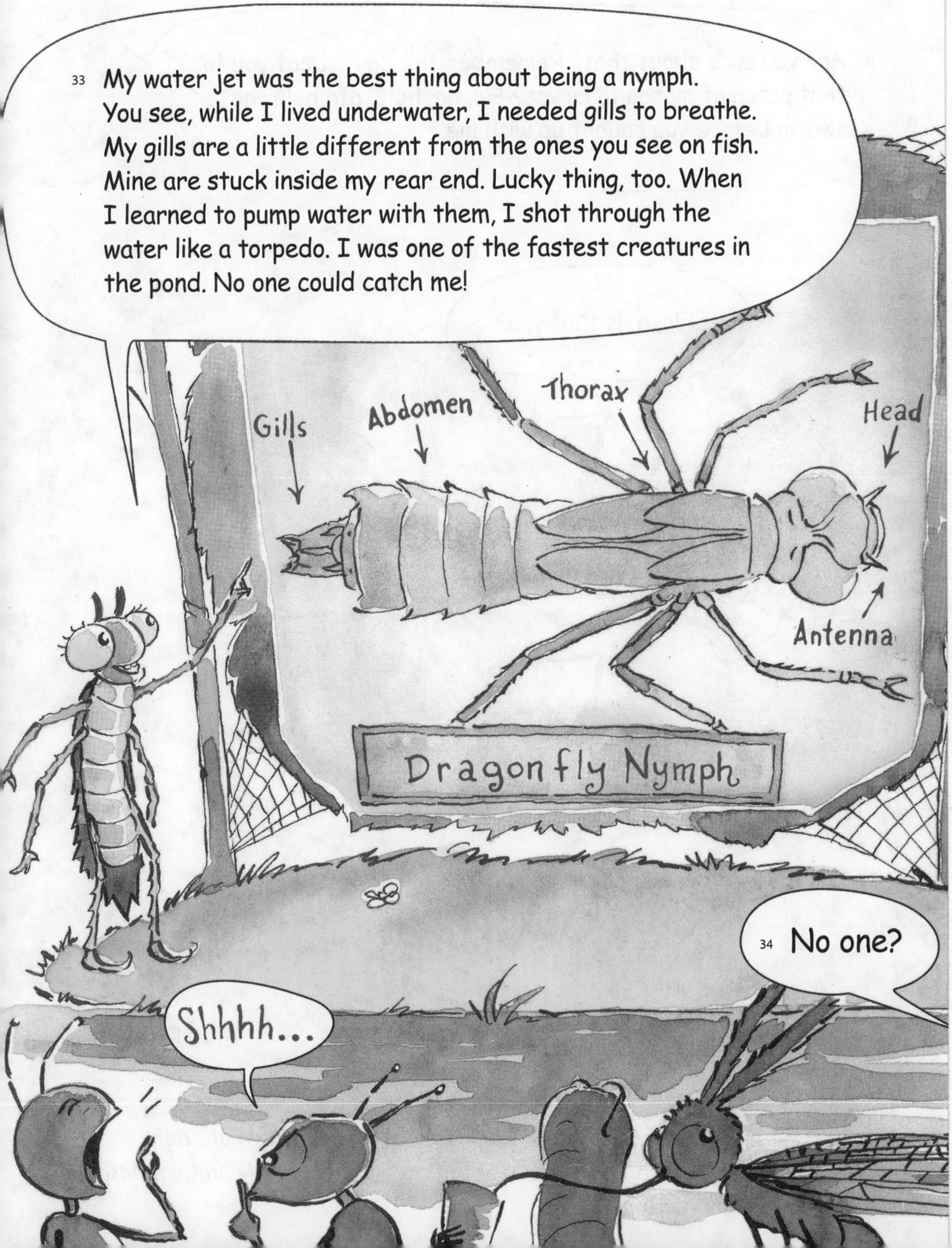

33 My water jet was the best thing about being a nymph. You see, while I lived underwater, I needed gills to breathe. My gills are a little different from the ones you see on fish. Mine are stuck inside my rear end. Lucky thing, too. When I learned to pump water with them, I shot through the water like a torpedo. I was one of the fastest creatures in the pond. No one could catch me!

Gills
Abdomen
Thorax
Head
Antenna

Dragonfly Nymph

Shhhh...

34 No one?

35 Are you sure about that? Remember the day I beat you to that patch of mosquito larvae? Ha, ha, ha! I ate half the swarm before you caught up with me.

36 Flash, is that you?

Mystery Guest #3

37 Yes, Dahlia, that's right.
It's your little brother, Flash.

38 Flash! I'm so excited, I popped my exoskeleton!

39 *It appears that Dahlia is splitting before our eyes. Flash, do you mind staying with us while she crawls out of that* **cumbersome** *exoskeleton?*

Split, Dahlia

40 Not at all, Bob. I can't wait to see the size of her wings.

GO FOR BROKE

cumbersome Something that is cumbersome is heavy and hard to carry or wear.

41 *Dahlia, are you okay? You look a bit pale and soft.*

42 I'll be fine, Bob. I just need some fresh air.

43 *Certainly, Dahlia. Take your time. I remember the day I molted into adulthood. My skin felt so tight. Then it began to split. I crawled out of my exoskeleton feeling a bit soft and dizzy. But after a few hours in the sun, I felt just fine.*

44 *Folks, while we wait for the blood to pump through Dahlia's wings, let's take a moment to hear from our BUG network sponsor, Bird-B-Gone.*

45 *Are you tired of being pecked and poked by killer birds?*

46 *Wish you could finish a meal without losing a body part?*

47 *If so, try new Bird-B-Gone! Produced by king crickets, this super-stinky spray could save your life.*

48 *Just a few squirts of Bird-B-Gone across your abdomen, and birds literally hit the sky.*

49 *Imagine stepping out of the cover of darkness and chomping your next leaf under the summer sun!*

50 *Get Bird-B-Gone, and get on with your life!*

39

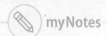

53 *Queens and grubs, take a look at those wings!*

54 Dahlia, is it true that your wings allow you to fly over 50 miles per hour?

55 Yes, Fly Guy, it's true. I'm one of the fastest insects on earth. And because I have four wings, I can fly forward, backward, and sideways. I can hover, dart, and flip through the air.

Ahhhh...

Ooooo...

56 *That's quite impressive, Dahlia. But why do you need such fancy flying skills?*

57 Well, Bob, I'm a hunter. I can catch and eat just about any type of insect I please.

58 *I hate to say it, folks, but we're running out of time. It appears that Dahlia is about to flutter away to watch her brothers and sisters emerge. And when that happens, we're all in danger of becoming their first meal.*

59 I'm sorry to chase you off like this, but you know how dragonflies are: Dash, dive, and destroy. Once we emerge, the only thing we want to do is eat, eat, eat. I must say, some of your audience members look absolutely delicious.

60 *You heard her, everyone. It's time for us to buzz off!*

61 *As the sun rises, a young dragonfly takes flight. Soon new dragonfly nymphs will wiggle through dangerous waters, where they will grow and molt into fast-flying adults. Thank you all for joining us for this fabulous event.*

GOOD-BYE, Dahlia!

BIRD GONE

62 *Until next time, this is Bob Beetle, saying: When the last egg is laid and it's your turn to sit down and die, just remember . . .*

THIS IS YOUR LIFE CYCLE!

Collaborative Discussion

Look back at what you wrote on page 18. Tell a partner what you learned about dragonflies. Then work with a group to discuss the questions below. Refer to details in *This Is Your Life Cycle* to explain your answers. Take notes for your responses.

1 Reread page 21. Why does the host say that Dahlia spent two years "fighting for her life"? How did she survive?

2 Review pages 40–43. What is Dahlia able to do once she has wings?

3 What parts of *This Is Your Life Cycle* are like things you might see or hear on a real television show?

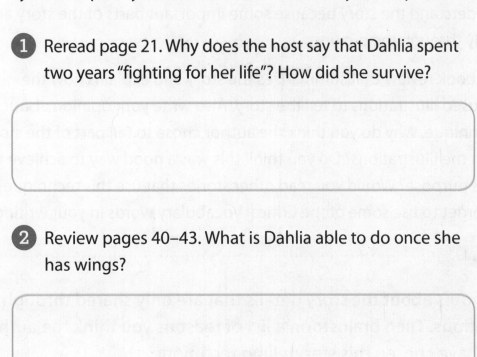

Listening Tip

Listen carefully to the comments of other group members. Try not to repeat what someone else has already said.

Speaking Tip

Be sure the ideas you share fit the topic. Don't talk about other things on your mind!

Write a Book Review

The author of *This Is Your Life Cycle* uses a make-believe TV show and humor to explain the stages in the life of a dragonfly. Unlike many stories, readers must pay careful attention to the details of each illustration to fully understand the story because some important parts of the story are told only through the pictures.

Write a book review that summarizes the story and explains how the author used illustrations to tell the story. Also write your opinion about this technique. Why do you think the author chose to tell part of the story through the illustrations? Do you think this was a good way to achieve the author's purpose? Would you read other stories that use this technique? Don't forget to use some of the Critical Vocabulary words in your writing.

PLAN

Make notes about the story details that are only shared through illustrations. Then brainstorm a list of reasons you think the author might have chosen this storytelling technique.

Now write your book review.

✓

Make sure your book review
☐ summarizes the plot.
☐ explains how the author uses pictures to tell part of the story.
☐ expresses your opinion of the author's choice to tell story details in pictures.
☐ contains facts and examples from the text to support your ideas.

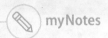

Notice &
Note
3 Big Questions

Prepare to Read

GENRE STUDY **Magazine articles** give information about a topic related to the publication's issue.

- Authors of magazine articles may organize their ideas using headings and subheadings.
- Authors of magazine articles may organize their writing around a central, or main, idea.
- Magazine articles include visuals, such as photographs, illustrations, maps, and diagrams.
- Science-based articles include words that are specific to the topic.

SET A PURPOSE **Think about** the title and genre of this text. What do you think this text is about? What would you like to learn from this text? Write your responses below.

CRITICAL VOCABULA

keener

nostrils

trumpet

**Build Background:
The Human Nose**

THE NOSE AWARDS

illustrated by
Manu Callejon

WHAT ANIMAL HAS THE MOST MAGNIFICENT NOSE?

1   Most people would say the elephant. An elephant uses its long nose, called a trunk, to breathe and smell. It also uses its nose to eat, drink, bathe, bellow, and more.

2   Other animals have nifty noses, too. Here we present the Elly, our very own nose award, to some of our favorite noses.

⭐ELLY BEST SMELLER

3   Elephants wave their long trunks back and forth, constantly checking the smells in every direction. They have a great sense of smell. They can pick up scents from several miles away.

These animals also deserve
Ellies for their super smelling skills.

4   People mostly use their eyes to learn
about the world. Dogs use their noses.
You might be able to see and count the
petals on a flower. A dog can smell
which petals were touched by a person
or an insect and how long ago.

5   A bear's sense of smell is even
keener than a dog's. Bears have poor
eyesight, but they can smell food from
miles away. They can even smell food
buried underground or packed inside an
unopened can.

> **keener**   If an animal's senses are keener, they
> are better, sharper, or more developed.

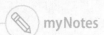

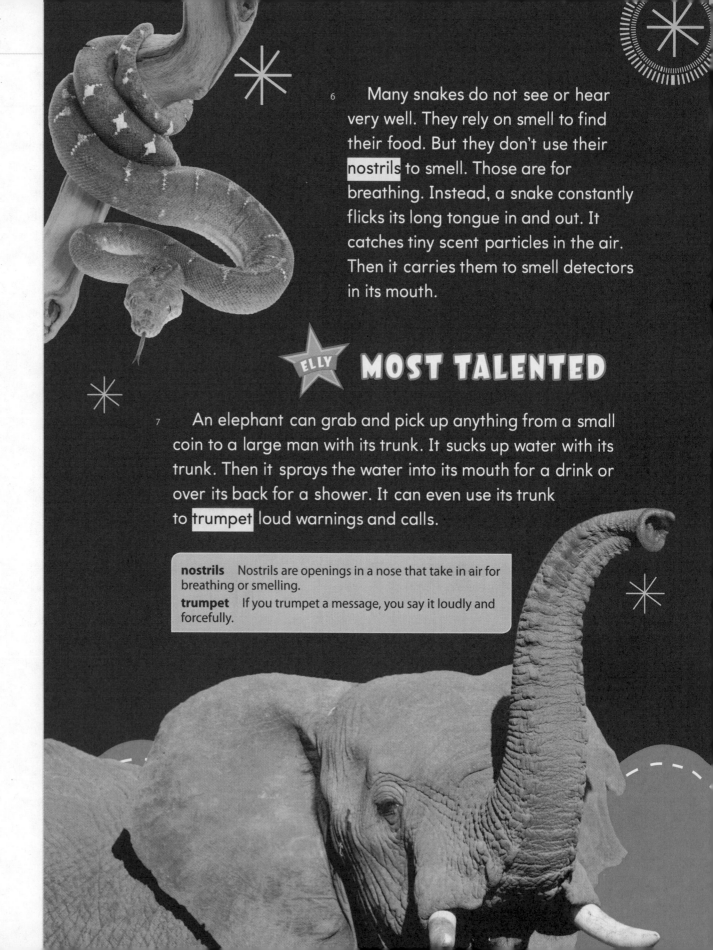

6   Many snakes do not see or hear very well. They rely on smell to find their food. But they don't use their nostrils to smell. Those are for breathing. Instead, a snake constantly flicks its long tongue in and out. It catches tiny scent particles in the air. Then it carries them to smell detectors in its mouth.

ELLY MOST TALENTED

7   An elephant can grab and pick up anything from a small coin to a large man with its trunk. It sucks up water with its trunk. Then it sprays the water into its mouth for a drink or over its back for a shower. It can even use its trunk to trumpet loud warnings and calls.

nostrils   Nostrils are openings in a nose that take in air for breathing or smelling.

trumpet   If you trumpet a message, you say it loudly and forcefully.

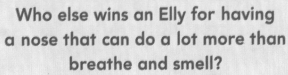

Who else wins an Elly for having a nose that can do a lot more than breathe and smell?

8   A pig uses its strong snout like a shovel to dig up tasty roots and bugs to eat.

9   A star-nosed mole has 22 pink "fingers" on its nose. Nearly blind, the mole tunnels underground, using those nose fingers, or tentacles, to feel for yummy worms and tiny bugs to eat.

BEST UNDERWATER

10 A swimming elephant keeps the tip of its trunk above the water. It uses its trunk like a snorkel or breathing tube.

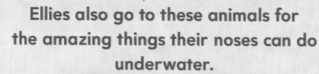

Ellies also go to these animals for the amazing things their noses can do underwater.

11 A hippopotamus spends most of the hot day in the water, where it's nice and cool. Breathing is not a problem because the hippo's nostrils face upward, sticking out of the water. If the hippo does go completely underwater, the nostrils shut tight.

12 Sharks breathe through their gills, so all their nostrils do is smell, all the time. The shark can compare how long it takes a smell to reach each nostril to figure out which direction the smell is coming from.

Collaborative Discussion

Look back at page 48. Share your responses with a partner. Then work with a group to discuss the questions below. Refer to details and examples in *The Nose Awards* to explain your answers. Take notes for your responses.

1 Reread page 51. Which award do dogs and bears win? Why do they win that award?

2 Review page 53. What is unusual about the star-nosed mole's nose?

3 What are some ways that animals' noses are different from people's noses?

Listening Tip

If you don't understand what someone else has said, ask a question to better understand.

Speaking Tip

Speak at a pace that isn't too fast or too slow and at a volume that everyone can hear.

Write an Announcement

In *The Nose Awards*, the author explains why several animals might be chosen to receive a special award called an "Elly."

Imagine that you have been asked to select one animal as the winner of the Elly award. Write an announcement to tell which animal you selected and why that animal's nose deserves the award. Since this is an award announcement, use words that are exciting and grab readers' attention. Try to use some of the Critical Vocabulary words in your writing.

PLAN ....

Make a list of facts and details from the story that explain why your favorite animal deserves to win the Elly award.

Now write your announcement to explain which animal is receiving the Elly award and why.

Make sure your announcement
☐ introduces the topic by announcing your choice.
☐ uses facts and details from the text to support your choice.
☐ uses exciting, attention-getting word choices.
☐ ends with a conclusion.

Notice & Note
3 Big Questions

Prepare to Read

GENRE STUDY **Narrative nonfiction** gives factual information by telling a true story.

- Narrative nonfiction presents events in sequential, or chronological, order.
- Authors of narrative nonfiction texts may include words that are specific to a science topic.
- Narrative nonfiction includes visuals, such as illustrations, maps, and diagrams.
- Narrative nonfiction may include text features, such as bold print, captions, and italics.

SET A PURPOSE **Think about** the title and genre of this text. What do you know about octopuses? What would you like to learn? Write your responses below.

CRITICAL VOCABULARY

flexible

siphon

lurking

invisible

Meet the Author and Illustrator:
Laurie Ellen Angus

Octopus Escapes Again!

Written and Illustrated
by Laurie Ellen Angus

1 Octopus is very hungry.
She peeks to the right.
Peeks to the left.
And dashes from her den into the deep, dark sea.

2 Will she eat today?
Or be eaten?

3 Those shrimp would make a tasty treat for her.

4 But far above, a sea turtle is looking for a tasty treat, too.

5 Spotting Octopus he dives down,
                        down,
                  down.

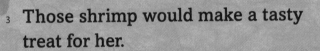

6   Quickly, Octopus
squeezes her soft body into
a nearby empty shell. A clever trick!

7   The turtle pushes,
  pokes,
    nudges,
      and noses—
        but Octopus is safe.

---

8   *Octopuses have no bones, which makes them very flexible. They sometimes squeeze their bodies into empty bottles, cans, and even coconut shells.*

flexible   If something is flexible, it can bend or change shape without breaking.

9 Octopus is still hungry. She swims
alongside a school of fish.

10 One of her eight long arms reaches
out to grab and gobble.

11 But wait!
Octopus spies an eel
slipping out of its cave,
ready to grab and gobble her!

12   **Whoosh! Octopus releases her secret weapon—a cloud of dark ink.**

13   **She scoots away, still hungry.**

---

14   *When threatened, an octopus can spray ink. This confuses the attacker and hides the octopus, giving it time to escape.*

15 Hunting for a shellfish or two, she glides
into nooks and slides into crannies.

16 But a prowling shark is hunting, too.
It spots Octopus and closes in.

17 **Luckily for Octopus she knows how to make a speedy getaway.**

18 **BLAST OFF!**

---

19 *When needing to make a fast escape, an octopus sucks in water and blasts it out through its siphon. The force of the water shoots the octopus away like a rocket.*

siphon   A siphon is a tube or hose that is used to pull liquid in or out.

20 Now Octopus is very hungry. She has a taste for snails.

21 But a giant grouper, **lurking** behind the sea grass, has a taste for Octopus. He opens his huge mouth wide to suck her in like a vacuum—hoping to swallow her in one giant gulp!

> **lurking**   If an animal is lurking, it is hiding while it waits to catch another creature.

22 **The grouper catches a
wriggling arm.
But only one!**

23 **Octopus escapes again!**

---

24 *When a predator catches an octopus by one of its
arms, an octopus can release it from its body. While the
predator is busy eating the arm, the octopus is
able to escape. The arm will eventually grow back.*

25 Still looking for a meal,
Octopus crawls into
shallow water along
the shoreline. Slowly she
sneaks in to grab a crab.

26   Uh-oh, a gull is swooping down.
     Is it after Octopus or a crab?
     Octopus doesn't wait to find out.

27   **POOF!**

28   Octopus disappears! She's a
     champion of camouflage.

29   Can you find her?

30   *When threatened, an octopus can instantly
     change its color and texture to blend into its
     surroundings. And it becomes completely
     invisible to an attacker.*

     invisible   If something is invisible, it cannot be seen.

31 Clams would make a savory supper.
She dives back down into the
deep, dark sea, reaches out,
and scoops some up.

32   Finally—it's time to eat!

Welcome to the Wonderful World of the Octopus

33 There are about 300 species of octopuses. Some are so small they can fit into the palm of your hand. The record for largest octopus, a Giant Pacific Octopus, is 30 feet. That's almost as long as a school bus.

34 Octopuses are found in all oceans of the world. Some live close to shore. Others live far out in the ocean.

35 The word *octopus* comes from two Greek words meaning "eight" and "foot." Octopuses have eight flexible arms that are made mostly of muscle.

36 Octopuses don't have any bones. The only hard part of an octopus is its beak, which is part of its mouth.

37 Octopuses like to be alone. They spend most of their time hiding in their den—their home. They often create a den under a pile of rocks, inside a cave, or in a crack of coral. Some octopuses have used empty shells or glass bottles as a den. They usually hunt for food at night.

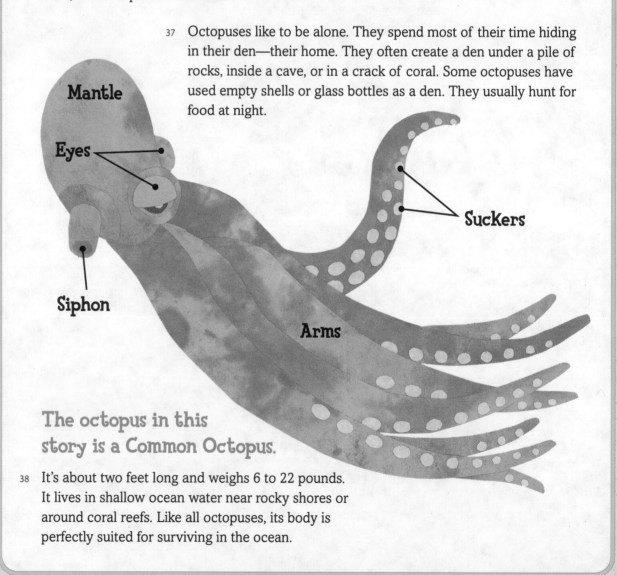

Mantle

Eyes

Siphon

Suckers

Arms

The octopus in this story is a Common Octopus.

38 It's about two feet long and weighs 6 to 22 pounds. It lives in shallow ocean water near rocky shores or around coral reefs. Like all octopuses, its body is perfectly suited for surviving in the ocean.

Collaborative Discussion

Look back at what you wrote on page 58. Tell a partner what you learned about octopuses. Then work with a group to discuss the questions below. Use details in *Octopus Escapes Again!* to explain your answers. Take notes for your responses.

1 Review pages 62–70. How can Octopus stay safe when another animal wants to eat it?

2 Reread pages 64–66. How is octopus ink like water shot from the octopus's siphon? How are the two different?

3 What kinds of fish does an octopus want to eat? Which animals want to eat an octopus?

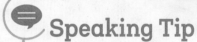

Listening Tip

Look at each speaker in your group. Show that you understand or agree with a smile or a nod.

Speaking Tip

If someone shares an idea that isn't quite clear, say what you think you heard. Use complete sentences, and ask, "Is that right?"

Write a Poem

In *Octopus Escapes Again!*, the main character must avoid predators while preying on other animals to eat. Clever Octopus uses many adaptations, such as camouflage and an ink cloud, to stay safe once again while searching for her dinner.

The author creates vivid images in readers' minds by using descriptive words to describe the animals' actions. For example, the author does not say the octopus eats a crab; instead she says Octopus "sneaks in to grab a crab." Readers can picture her quietly, patiently approaching the crab before she snatches it all of a sudden. Vivid word choices are often used in poetry, too. Write a poem that tells about Octopus's day, using your favorite descriptive action words from the story. Then add one or two original vivid descriptions of your own, too. Don't forget to use some of the Critical Vocabulary words in your writing.

PLAN

Make a list of words and phrases from *Octopus Escapes Again!* that create vivid images in your mind. Circle your favorites.

Now write your poem that tells about Octopus's day using vivid descriptions.

✔ Make sure your poem

☐ uses descriptive action words and vivid imagery found in the text.

☐ has at least one original vivid description of your own.

☐ demonstrates your understanding of the text.

☐ summarizes the events of Octopus's day.

Prepare to Read

GENRE STUDY **Informational texts** give facts and examples about a topic.

- Authors of informational texts may present their ideas in sequential, or chronological, order.
- Authors of informational texts may organize their ideas by stating a problem and explaining its solution, explaining causes and effects, and/or comparing and contrasting.
- Informational texts include visuals, such as charts, diagrams, graphs, timelines, and maps.

SET A PURPOSE **Think about** the title and genre of this text. What do you know about Tigers? What would you like to learn? Write your responses below.

CRITICAL VOCABULARY

nuzzled

bared

assistant

refused

nursery

pounce

Build Background: Siberian Tigers

T. J.
The Siberian Tiger Cub

By Ann Whitehead Nagda and Cindy Bickel

illustrated by Heather Gatley

T.J. plays with a ball.

1 Buhkra, the Siberian tiger, was going to have a baby. The keepers at the Denver Zoo had already placed a video camera in her den, so they could check on the mother tiger without disturbing her. When the cub was born, they watched Buhkra and her baby on a TV screen. Buhkra was a good mother. She licked, nuzzled, and nursed her new baby. The cub, named T.J., weighed only three pounds and looked tiny next to his mother, who weighed 250 pounds. T.J.'s father, Matthew, was even bigger than Buhkra. He weighed 350 pounds. T.J. would have to gain a lot of weight to be as big as his father.

nuzzled   If one animal nuzzled another animal, it gently touched the animal with its nose and mouth.

2   When T.J. was six weeks old, the zoo veterinarian gave him shots and weighed him. The cub weighed ten pounds. When T.J.'s father was six weeks old, he weighed fourteen pounds, four pounds more than T.J. Even so, the little tiger was healthy and strong. Sheila, the tiger keeper, had trouble holding him still while the vet examined him. The feisty little cub never stopped wriggling until Sheila brought him back to his mother.

3   Every day when Sheila came to the zoo, the first thing she did was check on the tigers. Buhkra, protecting her cub, always snarled, spit, and bared her teeth at Sheila. T.J. snarled just like his mother.

4   One morning, Buhkra didn't snarl at Sheila. The mother tiger lay on her side, completely still. T.J. was mewing and pushing his mother and trying to nurse, but Buhkra didn't move. Without any warning, she had died. The zoo veterinarian examined Buhkra and discovered she'd died from cancer.

5   Now who would raise this special baby? Most of the time, mother tigers take care of their cubs alone. Matthew couldn't take care of his son. He didn't know how.

bared   If an animal bared its teeth, it showed them in an angry way.

T.J. lays in his corner.

6   Sheila took T.J. to be raised by the staff at the animal hospital. The vet was worried when he examined the cub. T.J. was not as big as he should have been. The cub was ten weeks old and he weighed only thirteen pounds.

7   Cindy, a veterinary assistant at the hospital, put T.J. in a cage. She gave him a bowl of ground meat mixed with milk. Ignoring the food, T.J. walked to a corner of the cage, curled into a ball, and didn't move for hours. The next day he was still curled up in the same spot. He hadn't touched his food.

8   The hospital staff was worried. The ten-week-old cub hadn't gained much weight since his six-week checkup.

9   The vet checked to see how much T.J.'s father had weighed as a cub. He compared T.J.'s weight with Matthew's weight at the same ages. At six weeks, Matthew weighed four pounds more than T.J. At ten weeks, Matthew weighed six pounds more than T.J.

assistant   An assistant is someone who helps another person do his or her work.

10   It was T.J.'s third day at the hospital and he still hadn't eaten. When Cindy entered his cage, he snarled and showed his teeth. He threatened her because he was scared. She put some meat on a wooden stick and placed the meat in his mouth. T.J. spat it out.

11   The next day Cindy tried giving him strained meat from a jar. She thought that T.J. might like human baby food. He spat that out, too.

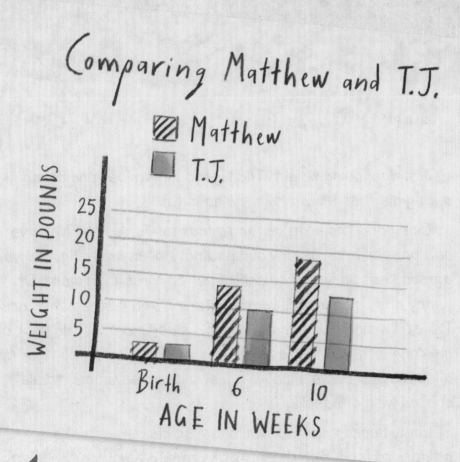

Cindy made a bar graph like this one to compare the tigers' weights. The red bars show T.J.'s weight. The black bars show Matthew's weight.

T.J. flattens his ears and snarls when he is frightened.

12   T.J. was losing weight. The tiger cub had lost one pound during his first few days in the hospital.

13   Cindy and the staff began to fear for T.J.'s life. Five days had passed and the tiny cub had not eaten anything. Everyone agreed that they had no choice but to force T.J. to eat. Dr. Kenny and Dr. Cambre, wearing jackets and heavy gloves, held T.J. still while Cindy used a stick to place meat at the back of his tongue. It was quite a struggle at first. The small tiger was all teeth and claws. Finally, T.J. swallowed seven meatballs coated with dried milk.

14   Cindy hoped that T.J. would eat on his own after he got a taste of food. But the cub still refused to touch the meat in his bowl. To help T.J. survive, Cindy and the veterinarians continued to force T.J. to eat.

refused   If you refused something, you did not take it.

Here is a line graph of both T.J.'s and Matthew's weight from birth to twelve weeks. The red line is T.J.'s weight. The black line is Matthew's weight. At twelve weeks, T.J. weighed a lot less than his father did at the same age.

The hospital staff monitor T.J.'s weight by creating a graph.

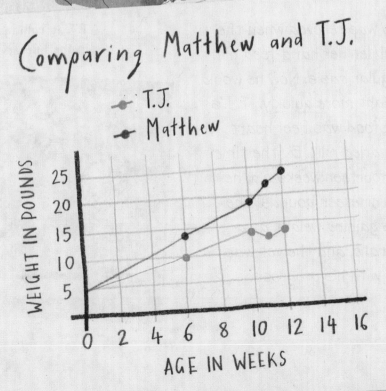

Comparing Matthew and T.J.

- T.J.
- Matthew

WEIGHT IN POUNDS

25
20
15
10
5

0 2 4 6 8 10 12 14 16

AGE IN WEEKS

15   On the eleventh day, T.J. ate two meatballs on his own. When Cindy gave the cub a rubber toy, he batted it around. Then she set a meaty bone next to the toy. T.J. immediately started chewing on the bone. Everyone started to feel more hopeful. All the care and hard work paid off. T.J. gained weight at last.

16   T.J. was weighed frequently. By thirteen weeks of age, the frisky cub was not cooperative about getting on a scale by himself. Cindy had to hold the tiger and step onto the scale. Together, Cindy and T.J. weighed 126 pounds. Cindy put the tiger down and stepped back onto the scale alone. It read 110 pounds. By subtracting her weight from their combined weight, Cindy was able to figure out that the tiger cub now weighed 16 pounds.

17   Cindy was relieved when the tiger cub let her hand-feed him on a regular basis. Now he would gain weight more quickly. T.J.'s favorite food was beef heart rolled in dried milk. By the time he was fourteen weeks old, he weighed nineteen pounds. The cub was gaining weight at a steady rate, and the vet was pleased with his progress.

T.J. is rolling around in the nursery.

18   As T.J. grew more comfortable with the nursery staff, he became more playful. He played hide-and-seek with Cindy and Denny, another veterinary assistant, on the zoo grounds at night. The tiger cub would hide in the bushes and wait patiently until Denny got close to him. Then he would leap out, grabbing Denny's leg with his paws. Sometimes he would sneak up behind Cindy and pounce on her. Tiger mothers teach their babies how to hunt by playing games like this.

Hungry T.J. opening
a fridge for his snack.

19   The tiger quickly learned to open the nursery room door, so he could join his human friends in the kitchen. He also learned to open the refrigerator door by pulling on the towel hanging there. One time T.J. even helped himself to a bag of meat. By the end of T.J.'s stay in the zoo hospital, he wanted company all the time. He cried when he was by himself.

nursery   A nursery is a place where babies or young children are cared for.
pounce   If you pounce, you jump on something suddenly and hold on to it.

20   After learning to live with humans, T.J. had a new challenge. He had to leave the hospital, return to the tiger exhibit in the zoo, and live by himself. Cindy visited him often. Sheila, the tiger keeper, hand-fed him so that he would get to know her. T.J. played games with Sheila. Sometimes he climbed on a rock and then pounced on her when she entered the exhibit.

T.J. is very eager to eat his meat.

21   T.J. was afraid to go outside in the tiger yard at first, so Sheila and Cindy went with him. Soon he was having a wonderful time. He shredded bark from trees and watched birds and zoo visitors.

22   During the next few years, T.J. grew a lot.

23   When T.J. was two years old, he was moved to a zoo in Billings, Montana. The zoo had a brand-new tiger exhibit, but no tigers. T.J. was just what they needed. He continued to thrive in his new home.

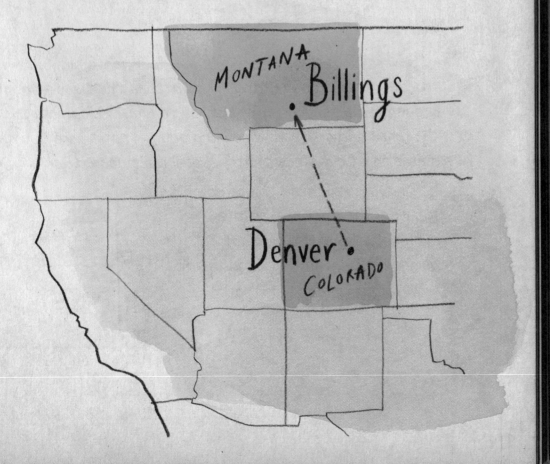

T.J.'s Big Move from Denver to Billings

MONTANA Billings

Denver
COLORADO

T.J. lays on his rock in Billings, Montana.

24   Several years later when T.J. was four years old, Cindy went to visit him at ZooMontana. She watched the tiger splash around in his pool. After she called to him, T.J. came over to the fence and chuffled, which is a sound that tigers use as a greeting. Cindy knew that T.J. still remembered her.

25   Cindy was amazed to see how big T.J. was. The tiger keeper at ZooMontana estimated that T.J. weighed 500 pounds. T.J. had finally grown bigger than his father!

Collaborative Discussion

Look back at page 76. Tell a partner what you learned about tigers. Then work with a group to discuss the questions below. Refer to details in *T.J. the Siberian Tiger Cub* to explain your answers. Take notes for your responses. Follow the rules for a polite discussion by taking turns, looking at your audience, and listening closely to others.

1 Review page 80. Why was the staff at the animal hospital worried about T.J?

2 Reread pages 81–82. What does Cindy do to try to get T.J. to eat? What does the tiger cub do?

3 What are some of the ways T.J. changes from the beginning of the selection to the end?

Listening Tip

Face the person who is talking. You can smile at the speaker and nod to show that you understand.

Speaking Tip

Choose a group leader who can call on one person at a time to speak. That person can make sure everyone will get a turn!

Write an Opinion Blog Entry

⋯⋯⋯⋯⋯⋯⋯⋯⋯⋯⋯⋯⋯⋯⋯⋯⋯⋯⋯⋯⋯⋯⋯⋯⋯

T.J. the Siberian Tiger Cub is a true story about a tiger cub born at the Denver Zoo. Many people worked hard to help him survive after his mother died.

Imagine that you write for the Denver Zoo's website. You have been asked to write about T.J. and his caregivers. Write a paragraph or two to tell what you think about his care based on the selection. What is the most important, or central, idea you want to tell readers about T.J.'s care? What part seems most difficult to you? What part seems like fun? Give reasons to support your opinion. Don't forget to use some of the Critical Vocabulary words in your writing.

PLAN ⋯⋯⋯⋯⋯⋯⋯⋯⋯⋯⋯⋯⋯⋯⋯⋯⋯⋯⋯⋯⋯⋯⋯⋯⋯⋯⋯⋯⋯⋯

In the headings of a two-column chart, list the hardest part of caring for T.J. and the most fun part. In each column, list facts and details from the text that support the heading.

WRITE

Now write your blog entry that states your opinions about T.J.'s care.

✓ **Make sure your blog entry**

☐ introduces the topic and states your opinion.
☐ provides reasons that support your opinion.
☐ uses linking words and phrases like *because*, *therefore*, and *for example* to connect opinions and reasons.
☐ provides a concluding statement.

(?) **Essential Question**

What behaviors help animals survive?

Write a Science Article

PROMPT Think about what you learned in this module about how animals survive.

Imagine that a science magazine for young people plans to focus on animal survival. You have been invited to write an article! Use evidence from the texts to explain one way that an animal's body or its actions help it to survive.

I will write about _____.

✓	**Make sure your science article**
☐	introduces the topic.
☐	includes facts, definitions, and details from the texts.
☐	presents information in a way that makes sense.
☐	uses linking words such as *also* and *but*.
☐	has a clear ending statement or conclusion.

PLAN ······························ **Gather information.**

What animal will you write about? What action or body parts will you explain? Look back at your notes and review the texts to help you choose.

The chart below will help you plan your article. Begin with a central idea sentence that states what you want to explain. Then find details in the texts that support your central idea. Use Critical Vocabulary words where you can.

My Topic: ______________________________

Central Idea

Detail	Detail	Detail

DRAFT ··· Write your article.

Use the information you wrote in the graphic organizer on page 93 to draft your article. Write an **introduction** that makes readers want to find out more about your topic.

State your central idea in a **body paragraph**. Add supporting details in each new sentence.

End your article with a sentence that reviews your main points.

The revision and editing steps give you a chance to look carefully at your writing and make changes. Work with a partner to determine whether you have explained your ideas clearly to readers. Use these questions to help you evaluate and improve your science article.

PURPOSE/ FOCUS	ORGANIZATION	EVIDENCE	LANGUAGE/ VOCABULARY	CONVENTIONS
☐ Do I state my topic clearly? ☐ Do I explain one way an animal is able to survive?	☐ Do I explain supporting details in a way that makes sense? ☐ Did I include an ending sentence that wraps up the article?	☐ Do I need to add more evidence to explain any of the details?	☐ Did I define science words that readers may not know?	☐ Are all words spelled correctly? ☐ Does each sentence have a subject and a verb? ☐ Did I use adjectives to describe or compare?

Create a Finished Copy Make a final copy of your article. You may want to include a photo or drawing to support your topic. Consider these options to share your article:

1. Combine your article with those of your classmates to make your own science magazine.

2. Work with a small group to plan a presentation for the class. Read aloud your articles and ask for comments and questions.

3. Record your article for a podcast on animal survival.

95

Make a Difference

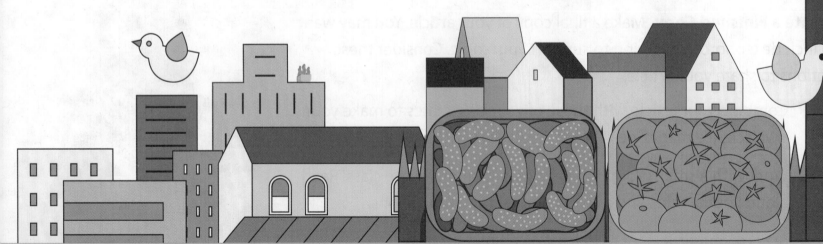

"Every individual matters.
Every individual has a role to play.
Every individual makes a difference."

—Jane Goodall

Essential Question

How can one person make a meaningful difference in their local or global community?

Get Curious
Video

Words About Making a Difference

The words in the chart below will help you talk and write about the selections in this module. Which words about making a difference in your community have you seen before? Which words are new to you?

Add to the Vocabulary Network on page 99 by writing synonyms, antonyms, and related words and phrases for each word.

After you read each selection in this module, come back to the Vocabulary Network and keep building it. Add more ovals if you need to.

WORD	MEANING	CONTEXT SENTENCE
outreach (noun)	When a program or people offer to help others in need, it is called outreach.	Samuel volunteers at a soup kitchen as part of his community outreach.
fellowship (noun)	A fellowship is a friendly feeling between people who share experiences.	A fellowship formed among the volunteers as they worked together.
communal (adjective)	Something is communal when it is shared by a group of people in the same community or area.	We take care of our plot in the communal garden.
residents (noun)	Residents of a house, city, or country are the people that live there.	The Johnsons are the residents of a home in the Bedford community.

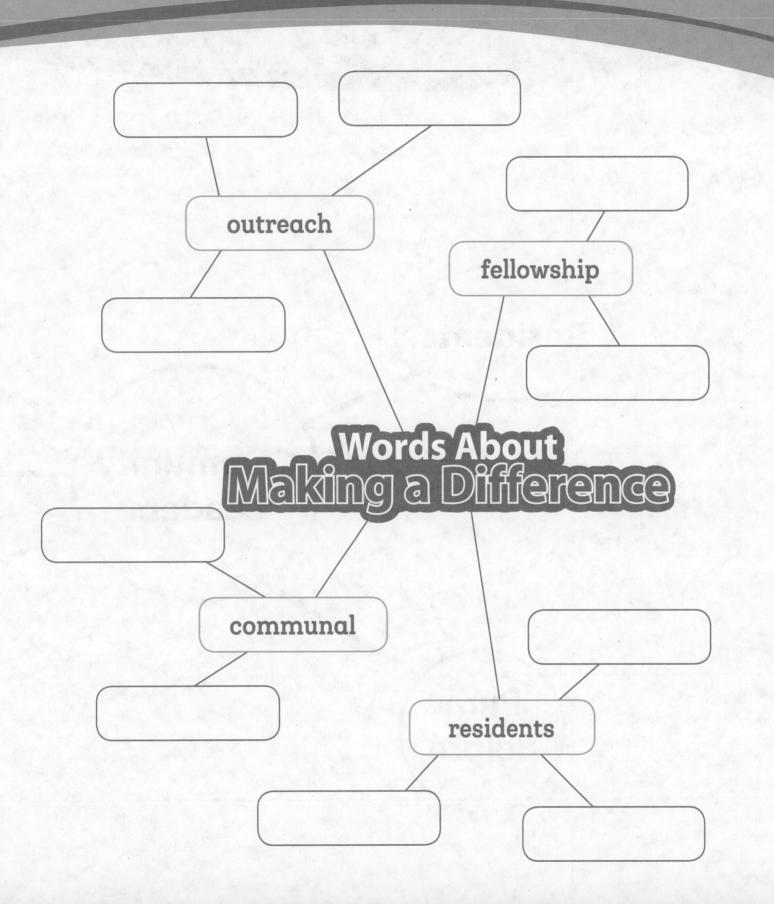

outreach

fellowship

Words About
Making a Difference

communal

residents

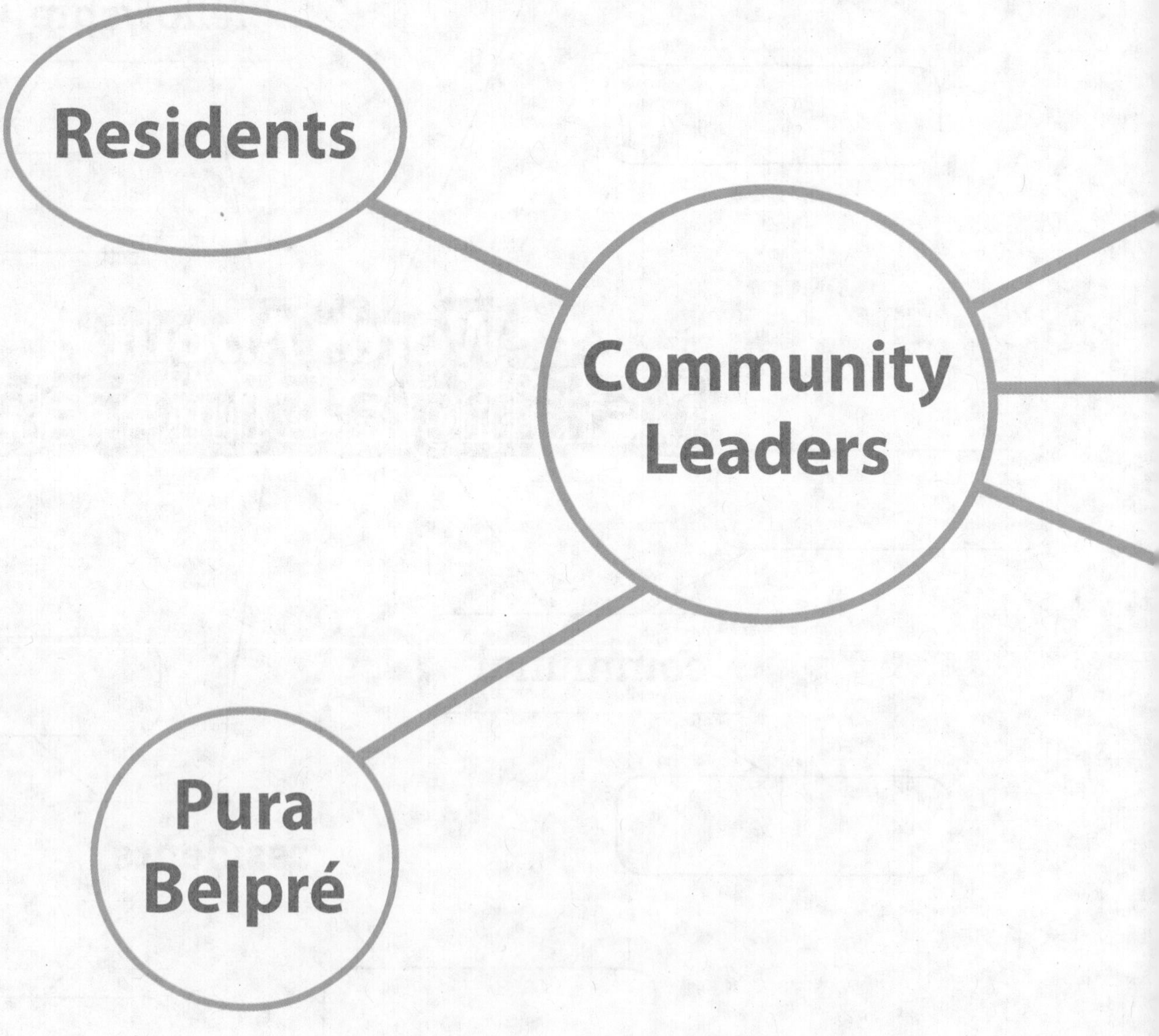

Residents

Community Leaders

Pura Belpré

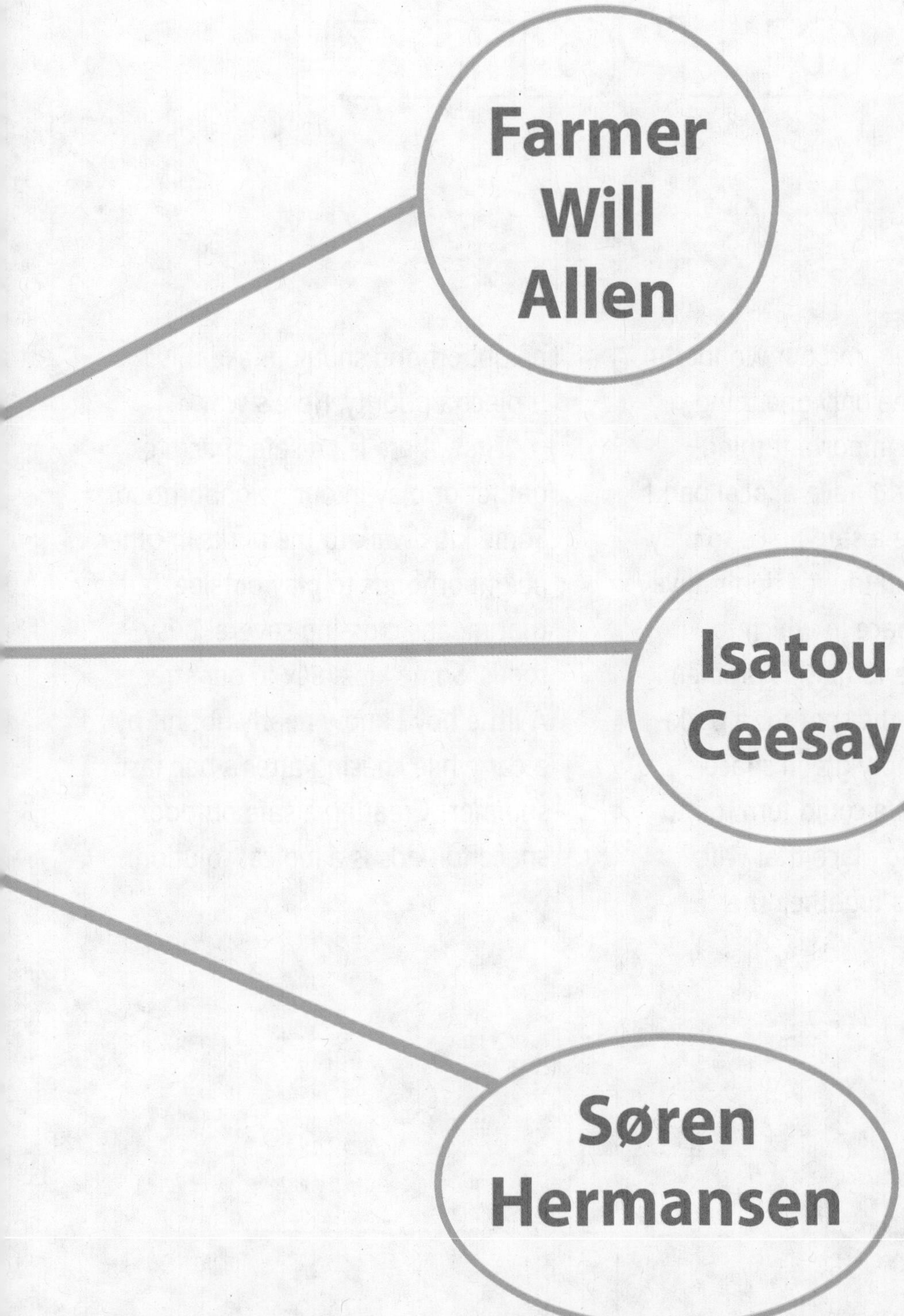

Farmer
Will
Allen

Isatou
Ceesay

Søren
Hermansen

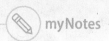

Let's Build a Park!

Lake

1　When I look around our wonderful community, I see only one thing missing. It's an important thing, though. We don't have a local park! Kids don't have a safe place to play, and families and friends don't have a communal space in which to gather. It's time to fix this problem.

2　I know just the spot for a park, too: the big empty green space near the lake. We could turn it into a safe gathering place that will bring neighbors together. The neighborhood should make this project a priority. Here's why.

3　First, there is no safe space to gather or play in our neighborhood. Some kids walk to the parks in other neighborhoods to play outside, but that means crossing several busy roads. Some kids play in our streets. A little boy I know nearly got hit by a car while chasing after a ball last summer! Creating a safe outdoor space for kids is a logical solution.

Dog Park

4   Second, the empty green space is ugly and dangerous. It's full of overgrown weeds, broken glass, and other trash. It's a real hazard to children and pets. Building a park there will change a trash heap into a place every resident can be proud of. Picture a green, shady place where grown-ups can relax, kids and dogs can play, and cats can . . . do whatever cats do. Sounds nice, doesn't it?

5   Finally, a new park will build fellowship in our community. Working toward a common goal can really bring people together. Sophie and Kendall Vu, new residents, told me they helped build a park in their last neighborhood. "Before the project, people hardly knew each other," Sophie says. "Then we worked together, and we all got to be great friends!"

6   I'll be doing outreach around the neighborhood next week. If you support a new park and want to help make it happen, please sign my petition. Let's all work together to make our community safer, friendlier, and more fun!

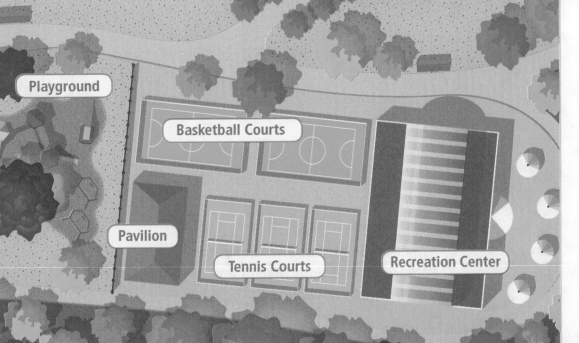

Gazebo

Playground

Basketball Courts

Pavilion

Tennis Courts

Recreation Center

Notice & Note
Quoted Words

Prepare to Read

GENRE STUDY ▶ A **biography** is the story of a real person's life written by someone other than that person.

- Authors of biographies present events in order.
- Authors of biographies may organize their ideas using headings.
- Biographies may include illustrations that show important events in the person's life.

SET A PURPOSE ▶ **Look at** the headings, illustrations, and words that stand out on each page. What do they tell you about farmer Will Allen? What would you like to learn about farmer Will and his growing table? Write your ideas.

Meet the Author and Illustrator:
Jacqueline Briggs Martin and
Eric-Shabazz Larkin

CRITICAL VOCABULARY

scarce

greenhouses

pollution

crowded

vats

vertical

factories

Farmer Will Allen and the GROWING TABLE

WRITTEN BY Jacqueline Briggs Martin   ILLUSTRATED BY Eric-Shabazz Larkin

FARMER WILL ALLEN

1 Farmer Will Allen is as tall as his truck. He can hold a cabbage—or a basketball—in one hand. When he laughs, everyone laughs, glad to be in his crew. When he talks, everyone listens.

2 But some say the special thing about Will Allen

is that **HE CAN SEE WHAT OTHERS CAN'T SEE.**

Are they right?

When he looked at an abandoned city lot

and saw a huge table heaped with food, was he right?

THE KITCHEN TABLE

3 When Will Allen was a boy bowls of peas, greens, and his favorite—lima beans with ham— covered the kitchen table.

4 "My mother often fixed enough food for thirty," Will says. "We never had a car or a TV, but we always had good food." He remembers people who'd come to dinner tired and drooped—

and leave LAUGHING.

5 Will's family grew most of their food. Will loved the food but hated the work.

6 He planned to quit on **PLANTING**, **PICKING**, **PULLING WEEDS**, leave those Maryland fields for basketball or white-shirt work.

7 And he did. He graduated from college and moved to Belgium to play professional **BASKETBALL**.

8 When a Belgian friend asked him to help dig potatoes Will realized he "loved digging in the dirt."

HE GREW SO MUCH FOOD

that he and his wife Cyndy covered their kitchen table with Thanksgiving dinner for a team of basketball friends.

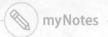
A NEW KIND OF FARM

9 When Will was done with basketball, he worked a white-shirt job in Wisconsin and found time to grow vegetables on Cyndy's parents' land.

10 But Will wanted his own place. He'd seen that fresh vegetables were as scarce in the city as trout in the desert. Will believed everyone, everywhere,

had a RIGHT to good food.

scarce   If something is scarce, there is very little of it.

11 **BUT HOW** could Will farm in the middle of
pavement and parking lots **?**

12 One day, driving in Milwaukee, Will spotted six empty
greenhouses on a plot of land about the size of a large
supermarket, FOR SALE!

13 He could see kids, who'd never eaten a ripe tomato,
never crunched a raw green bean, sitting at his table,
eating his vegetables. Will Allen bought that city lot!

greenhouses Greenhouses are glass
buildings that are used to grow plants and
protect them from the weather.

111

14 **W**ill had a start on his table. He had the land. But the table was empty. The problem was Will's soil—"dirty" with chemicals and pollution. He had no money for machines to dig out the bad soil, for truckloads of good soil.

WHAT TO DO?

15 In Belgium, Will had learned to make good soil with food garbage. They called it composting. But he needed lots of garbage. He asked his friends to save food waste—apple peels to old zucchinis.

16 Will collected those scraps in big white buckets and dumped them into piles.

17 He added hay, leaves, newspapers, red wiggler **WORMS**, water. Every now and then he turned the piles to get air into the mix. Neighborhood kids stopped by to ask what he was doing.

18 Will told them about the piles and the red wiggler worms that would help the garbage become compost. The kids came back day after day to help.

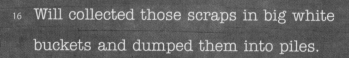

pollution Pollution is harmful or poisonous material in the air, water, and ground.

19   Then one day—bad news:

THE RED WIGGLER CREW WAS DYING.

20   Will and the kids studied worms for five years. They

learned not to feed the worms too much. And they

discovered the best menu for red wigglers:

no hot peppers, onions, garlic; lots

of watermelon rinds, sweet potato

scraps, molasses.

Since then the squirmy crew has stayed hard at work.

Will says worm "magic" is what makes his farm grow.

MAKING A BIGGER TABLE: GROWING POWER

21 Once Will had good soil, he was ready to plant vegetables. But he didn't have much space. How could he **GROW ENOUGH FOOD** on a small city plot **?**

22 Will Allen looked around. He saw that he had *all* the space from the soil under his feet to the top of the greenhouses.

23 He hung plant baskets from the ceiling. He grew greens in buckets, greens in rows. He crowded shelves with pots of spinach, chard, lettuce. He grew stacks of tiny salad sprouts in boxes, hundreds of boxes.

24 Will added hoophouses to hold more boxes and more long rows of vegetables. He added vats of water and fish to his greenhouses. Fish wastewater grows the sprouts. The sprouts clean the water for the fish.

FISH, WATER, SPROUTS WORK TOGETHER like a three-part **FARM MACHINE**.

25 He added goats, chickens, turkeys, and bees to that city farm he named "Growing Power."

crowded   If you crowded a space with something, you filled it up with no room left for anything else.

vats   Vats are large tanks or tubs that can hold water or other liquids.

26   Farmer Will's work clothes are jeans and a blue sweatshirt
with cutoff sleeves. He's busy from early morning to night.
      Still, one person could never grow all the food Will wanted to
grow. Where could he find more farmers in the middle of the city?

27   Will Allen looked around.

He saw teenagers, schoolchildren, parents, grandparents.

HE TAUGHT THEM TO BE FARMERS.

Then Will's "table" held as much as several supermarkets—
thousands of pounds of food.

28   Neighbors who live in high-rises, far off the growing ground, came—
and still come—to Will's farm to buy fresh vegetables, fish, or eggs.

People have gone—and still go—
to fancy restaurants to eat Will's food.

29   But Will wanted his table to feed folks all over the world.

          How could he build one HUGE
                                        table that
              crossed continents?

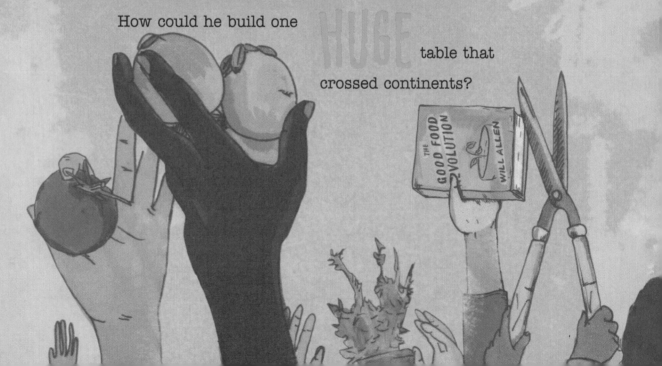

GROWING POWER
AROUND THE WORLD

30 Will thought about the problem of the world-sized table. He looked around and saw his many helpers who'd learned to be farmers. He would teach people **EVERYWHERE** to grow food for their own tables.

31 Will Allen began to travel.

He has crisscrossed the United States showing others how to farm in the city. And he has taken his red wigglers to Kenya, to London— **ALL OVER THE WORLD**.

32 The world has also come to his Milwaukee farm. Twenty thousand visitors a year tour the greenhouses, watch goats, snack on greens, and go home planning to **START A FARM** on a city lot, rooftop, or abandoned highway.

WILL AND THE FIFTY MILLION

33 Is Will Allen done? **NEVER!**

34 "We need fifty million more people growing food on porches, in pots, in side yards," he says. Will is always looking for new ways to make the table bigger—more schoolyard plots, a vertical farm that's five stories high, farms in empty factories or warehouses.

35 Will Allen dreams of a day when city farms are as common as streetlights, and EVERY TABLE IS COVERED WITH GOOD FOOD.

YOUR TABLE

36 **W**ill Allen can see what others can't see. When he sees kids, he sees farmers.

37 Will you be on Will Allen's crew? Will you grow vegetables for your family, your neighbors, on your porch, or roof, or yard?

38 How big will **YOUR** table be?

---

vertical Something that is vertical stands tall or points up.
factories Factories are large buildings where things are built or made by people and machines.

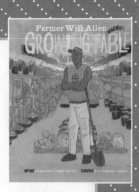

Collaborative Discussion

Look back at page 104. Tell a partner two things you learned. Then work with a group to discuss the questions below. Use details from *Farmer Will Allen and the Growing Table* to support your ideas. Take notes for your responses.

1 Reread pages 109–111. What are some reasons farmer Will Allen wanted to start a farm on the land with old, empty greenhouses?

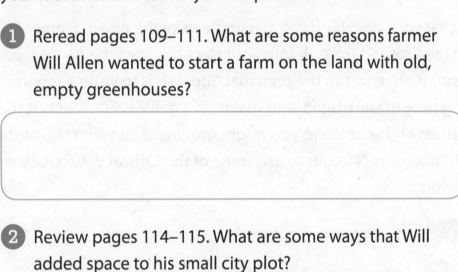

2 Review pages 114–115. What are some ways that Will added space to his small city plot?

3 What examples support the author's idea that Will "can see what others can't see"?

Listening Tip

Listen carefully to each speaker's examples and ideas. Could you tell what each speaker said in your own words?

Speaking Tip

If you are unclear about a speaker's idea, ask the speaker to tell you more to help you understand.

Write a How-To Report

PROMPT ....

In *Farmer Will Allen and the Growing Table*, you read about how Will Allen created a garden in the city. He had to be creative with his planning and encountered some problems along the way.

Imagine that your class is planning a garden like the one in *Farmer Will Allen and the Growing Table*. Before your class can start the garden, you need to submit a report to the principal. Your job is to write a report explaining how to start, build, and maintain a garden. Think about the types of fruits and vegetables you might grow, and consider the problems you might have. Don't forget to use some of the Critical Vocabulary words in your writing.

PLAN ....

Make notes about the problems farmer Will Allen encountered and how he solved them as he created his garden.

Now write your report about how to create and maintain your class garden.

✓ **Make sure your how-to report**

☐ begins by introducing your topic.

☐ includes facts and details from the text to support your

☐ uses transition words to connect steps in the process.

☐ ends with a concluding sentence.

Notice & Note
Aha Moment

Prepare to Read

GENRE STUDY A **biography** is the story of a real person's life written by someone other than that person.

- Authors of biographies present events in sequential, or chronological, order.
- Biographies may tell how real people felt about events described in the text.
- Biographies include third-person pronouns such as *he, she, him, her, his, hers, they, them,* and *their.*

SET A PURPOSE **Think about** the title of the biography. This story is about Isatou Ceesay. What would you like to learn from her story? Write your ideas below.

Meet the Author and Illustrator:
Miranda Paul and Elizabeth Zunon

CRITICAL VOCABULARY

confesses

forage

recycled

ONE PLASTIC BAG

ISATOU CEESAY AND THE RECYCLING WOMEN OF THE GAMBIA

MIRANDA PAUL

ILLUSTRATIONS BY

ELIZABETH ZUNON

Njau, Gambia

1   Isatou walks with her chin frozen. Fat raindrops pelt her bare arms. Her face hides in the shadow of a palm-leaf basket, and her neck stings with every step.

2   Warm scents of burning wood and bubbling peanut stew drift past. Her village is close now. She lifts her nose to catch the smell.

3   The basket tips.

4   One fruit tumbles.

5   Then two.

6   Then ten.

7   The basket breaks. Isatou kicks the dirt.

8   Something silky dances past her eyes, softening her anger. It moves like a flag, flapping in the wind, and settles under a tamarind tree. Isatou slides the strange fabric through her fingers and discovers it can carry things inside. She gathers her fruits in the bag.

9   The basket is useless now. She drops it, knowing it will crumble and mix back in with the dirt.

10   Four goats greet Isatou as
Grandmother Mbombeh emerges
from her kitchen hut. "Hurry in before
the rain soaks your beautiful *mbuba*!"

11   Isatou scurries in, and Grandmother serves spicy rice and
fish. Rain drums on the creaking aluminum roof.

12   "I . . . broke your basket," Isatou confesses. "But I found this."

13   "Plastic," Grandmother frowns. "There's more in the city."

> **confesses**   If someone confesses something, he or
> she admits to doing or saying something wrong.

14 Day after day, Isatou watches neighbors tote their things in bright blue or black plastic bags. Children slurp water and *wanjo* from tiny holes poked in clear bags. Market trays fill with *minties* wrapped in rainbows of plastic.

15 The colors are beautiful, she thinks. She swings her bag high. The handle breaks.

16 One paper escapes.

17 Then two.

18 Then ten.

19 Isatou shakes sand off her papers. Another plastic bag floats by, and she tucks her things inside.

20 The torn bag is useless now. She drops it to the dirt, as everyone does. There's nowhere else to put it.

21   Day after day, the bag she dropped is still there. One plastic bag becomes two.

22   Then ten.

23   Then a hundred.

24   Plastic isn't beautiful anymore, she thinks. Her feet step down a cleaner path, and the thought floats away.

25   Years pass and Isatou grows into a woman. She barely notices the ugliness growing around her . . .

      until the ugliness finds its way to her.

26   Isatou hears a goat crying and hurries toward Grandmother's house. Why is it tied up? Where are the other goats?

27   Inside, the butcher is speaking in a low voice.

28   "Many goats have been eating these," he says. "The bags twist around their insides, and the animals cannot survive. Now three of your goats and so many other goats in the village have died!"

29   Grandmother Mbombeh's powerful shoulders sag. Isatou must be strong and do something. But what?

30   Isatou's feet lead her to the old, ugly road. A pile of garbage stands as wide as Grandmother's cooking hut. Mosquitoes swarm near dirty pools of water alongside the pile. Smoke from burning plastic stings her nose. Her feet back away.

31   Goats scamper past. They **forage** through the trash for food. Her feet stop. She knows too much to ignore it now.

32   Holding her breath, she plucks one plastic bag from the pile.

33   Then two.

34   Then ten.

35   Then a hundred.

forage   When animals forage, they search through an area to find food.

131

36   "What can we do?" Isatou asks her friends.

37   "Let's wash them," says Fatim, pulling out *omo* soap.
Maram grabs a bucket, and Incha fetches water from
the well. Peggy finds clothespins, and they clip the
washed bags on the line.

38   As the bags dry, Isatou watches her sister crochet. "Can you teach me?"

39   "*Waaw*—yes." Her sister shows Isatou the stitches, then hands her a metal tool. Isatou's fingers busy themselves . . . in . . . out . . . around. "*Jerejef*—thank you."

40   Isatou finds a broomstick and carves her own tool from its wood.

41   "What's that for?" Fatim asks.

42   Isatou pauses. She and Peggy have an idea. But will their friends think it's crazy? Will the idea even work?

43   Nervously, she explains the plan.

44 One friend agrees to help.

45 Then two.

46 Then five!

47 The women cut bags into strips and roll them into spools of plastic thread. Before long, they teach themselves how to crochet with this thread.

48 "*Naka ligey be*?" asks Grandmother. "How is the work?"

49 "*Ndanka, ndanka*," answers Isatou. "Slow. Some people in the village laugh at us. Others call us 'dirty.' But I believe what we are doing is good."

50 The women crochet by candlelight, away from those who mock them . . . until a morning comes when they will no longer work in secret.

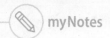

51   Fingers sore and blistered, Isatou hauls the recycled
purses to the city.

52   One person laughs at her.

53   Then two.

54   Then ten.

55   Then . . .

recycled   When something is descibed as recycled, it has been used again or used in a different way.

56   One woman lays dalasi coins on the table. She chooses a
purse and shows it to one friend.

57   Then two.

58   Then ten.

59   Soon everyone wants one!

60   Isatou fills her own purse with dalasi.
She zips it shut and rides home to tell Grandmother
she has made enough to buy a new goat.

61   When she passes by the pile of rubbish, she smiles
because it is smaller now. She tells herself, one day it
will be gone and my home will be beautiful.

62   And one day . . .

63 . . . it was.

Author's Note

64   I first traveled to the Gambia, West Africa, in 2003 as a volunteer teacher. I had an amazing experience, but something threatened to ruin my memory of it all—the heaps of garbage piled everywhere.

65   The problem seemed too big to fix. Then a friend told me that in a rural village a woman named Isatou Ceesay was doing something about it. My friend showed me a beautiful purse made from recycled plastic bags, and I vowed to meet Isatou.

66   During my third stay in the Gambia, in 2007, I finally connected with Isatou and visited her home in Njau. There I interviewed many women and girls, including the original Gambian women who had begun the recycling project with Isatou a decade earlier. They shared past stories of dead livestock, strangled gardens, and malaria outbreaks linked to the trash. But they also shared new stories of healthier families, better income, and increased self-confidence. Although I wasn't able to include all the details about the women and their project in this book, I believe the story I've shaped captures their spirit and inspirational accomplishments.

67   Today Njau is much cleaner, the goats are healthier, and the gardens grow better. Residents from nearby towns travel there to learn the craft of recycling. People from around the world continue to purchase the recycled plastic purses, and the women contribute some of their earnings toward an empowerment center where community members enjoy free health and literacy classes, as well as learn about the dangers of burning plastic trash.

68   In 2012, that center also became the home for the region's first public library. By the time you read this story, I hope that a copy of *One Plastic Bag* is shelved there and that it will be checked out once . . . then twice . . . then a hundred times!

Collaborative Discussion

Look back at what you wrote on page 122. Tell a partner two things you learned. Then work with a group to discuss the questions below. Use examples from *One Plastic Bag* to support your ideas. Come to the discussion prepared.

1. Reread pages 125–128. In what ways are plastic bags useful? What problem do the bags create?

2. Review pages 134–136. Why is the task of making the purses difficult for Isatou and her friends?

3. How does Isatou's recycling project help her family and her community?

Listening Tip

Give each speaker your full attention. Wait until he or she has finished talking before adding your own ideas.

Speaking Tip

If you disagree with someone, do it in a kind way. Point out details and examples in the text that led you to a different answer.

Write a Newspaper Article

In *One Plastic Bag*, you read about a woman who sees a problem and finds a creative solution. She and her friends turn trash into something useful.

Imagine you work for a newspaper and you are going to write an article about Isatou. What questions would you ask her in order to prepare for your article? Based on the text, how would she answer? What advice would she give to others? Write an article in which you describe Isatou's problem and the creative way she solved it. Include imaginary quotes from Isatou.

Write the problem Isatou encounters and how she solves it. Include questions for Isatou and ideas about how she might answer them.

Now write your newspaper article about Isatou and her creative
solution.

Make sure your article

☐ begins with an introduction.

☐ describes Isatou's problem and solution.

☐ includes details and examples from the text.

☐ uses linking words and phrases to connect ideas.

☐ includes imaginary quotes from Isatou.

☐ includes a concluding statement.

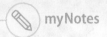

**Notice &
Note**
Aha Moment

Prepare to Read

> **GENRE STUDY** **Narrative nonfiction** gives factual information by telling a story.

- Narrative nonfiction presents events in order.
- Texts about events that happened in the past include real people.
- Narrative nonfiction texts about science include words that are specific to the topic and visuals, such as illustrations, maps, and diagrams.

> **SET A PURPOSE** **Think about** the title and illustration on the next page. What would you like to learn about Energy Island and how the island's community uses wind? Write your ideas below.

Meet the Author and Illustrator:
Allan Drummond

CRITICAL VOCABULARY

cable

environmental

renewable

converted

resources

willing

allan drummond
energy

island

How One Community Harnessed the Wind and Changed Their World

1   Welcome to Energy Island! The real name of our island is Samsø, but we like to call it "Energy Island."

2   Not too long ago we were just ordinary people living on an ordinary island in the middle of Denmark. In many ways, Samsø was—and still is—not very different from where *you* live. We have lots of fields and farms, where farmers raise cows and sheep, and grow crops like potatoes, peas, corn, and strawberries. And there is a harbor where the ferry and fishing boats come in.

3   Our little home has recently become quite famous, and scientists travel from all over the world just to talk to us and learn about what we've done. Why is that? Well, it's an interesting story.

4   Let's go! Hold on to your hats!

5   Our island is in the middle of Denmark, and it's in the middle of the sea. That's why it's always very windy here!

6   In the summer we have fun at the beach. And in the winter we play games inside.

7   We have villages and schools. Kids play soccer, and grownups go to the grocery store. It's very ordinary here—apart from the wind.

8 The way we used to use energy was very ordinary, too. On dark winter nights we switched on lots of lights and turned up our heaters to keep warm. We used hot water without even thinking. Our oil arrived by tanker ship and truck, and we used it to fill up our cars and our heating systems. And our electricity came from the mainland by cable under the sea.

> **cable**   A cable is a bundle of wires with a thick covering that is used to carry electricity.

9   A few years ago, most of us didn't think much about where our energy came from, or how it was made.

10   That was before our island won a very unusual competition. The Danish Ministry of Environment and Energy chose Samsø as the ideal place in Denmark to become independent of nonrenewable energy. A teacher named Søren Hermansen was selected to lead the energy independence project. He was a very ordinary person, too . . .

11   Okay, he did play bass guitar in a band. But his favorite subject was environmental studies. And he was very excited about energy independence. "Tell me, class, what are some ways we could make our own energy, right here on the island?"

Capture heat from the sun!

environmental   Something that is environmental is connected to protecting Earth's land, water, animals, and air.

Ride bicycles instead of driving cars!

Use oil from crops!

Burn straw and wood!

Renewable Energy

Renewable energy comes from resources that will never run out, or that can be replaced. For example, wind is a renewable resource, since the wind will always blow. Windmills were invented to catch that energy.

Rivers keep flowing all year, so they are also a source of renewable energy. People have been using dams, water mills, and other means of harnessing water power for thousands of years.

Sunlight, which can be converted into solar power, is another example of a renewable resource, and so are the plants and trees that can be harvested and converted into *biofuels* and then replanted.

Scientists are even figuring out how to create energy from burning garbage and human sewage!

renewable Something that is renewable will always be available.

converted When something is converted, it is changed to a different form or changed in some important way.

12   "Imagine if we really could make enough energy from the sun, and our crops, and even our own legs, to power up the whole island! Then we wouldn't need the oil tankers to come here. We wouldn't have to worry about all the world's oil running out. And we wouldn't need electricity to be sent from the mainland. Renewable resources are so much cleaner. And think of the money we'd save! We just need to think big."

13   "But do you think we can really create that much energy ourselves?" asked Naja. "From just the sun, our crops, and our legs?"

14   "Well, you know," said Kathrine, "if there's one thing our island has plenty of, it's wind. Maybe we should start with wind energy."

15   "That's a wonderful idea!" said Mr. Hermansen. "Who's with me?"

16   "Hold on to your hats!" we all said.

17   We kids were very excited about all the new ideas. But as for the grownups . . . Well, it took them a while to catch on.

resources The materials or things that people can use to get a job done are resources.

18 "It will cost millions!" said Jørgen Tranberg. "All these cows keep me busy enough already."

19 "Heat from the sun?" said Peter Poulen. "Why would we bother with that? As long as I can keep my house warm and watch TV, I'm happy. I don't need change."

20 "Bicycles?" said Mogens Mahler. "No way. I love my truck!"

21 "Why us?" said Dorthe Knudsen. "Let some other island take on the challenge."

22 "Renewable energy?" said Jens Hansen. "I'm too old for all that."

23 "Samsø is just an ordinary kind of place," said Ole Jørgensen. "What difference can we make to the world?"

24 "Energy independence? In your dreams!" said Petra Petersen.

25   But Søren Hermansen wouldn't give up. He called lots of local meetings. "There's energy all around us!" he told the islanders. "We just need to work together and think big to make the best use of it."

154

26   He talked to everyone . . .

The soccer team.

All the teachers.

The farmers at market.

The police.

The fishermen.

The lighthouse keeper.

The harbormaster.

The dentist.

27   This went on for several years. People listened, and lots of them even agreed with what Søren Hermansen was saying, but nothing happened. Was anyone willing to make a change?

> **willing**   If you are willing to do something, you are ready to do it.

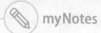

28 Then one day, the electrician Brian Kjær called Søren Hermansen. "I'm thinking small," he said. "I'd like to put up a secondhand wind turbine next to my house."

29 Jørgen Tranberg was thinking big. "I want a huge wind turbine. I'll invest my money and then sell the electricity it makes."

30 Mr. Hermansen was excited. Two renewable energy projects had begun. One very small and one very big!

31 Brian Kjær called on his family and friends to help him put up his wind turbine, while it took a big ship, some giant trucks, and two enormous cranes to build Jørgen Tranberg's!

32 The project on Samsø had begun, but we were still using a lot of nonrenewable energy. It looked like we might never achieve our dream. Until one dark winter night . . .

33   Sleet and snow blasted across the island. Suddenly, all the electricity on the entire island went out! Everything was dark.

34   Everything, that is, except Brian Kjær's house. "Free electricity!" shouted Mr. Kjær. "My turbine works! Tonight I'm energy-independent!" Sure enough, the blades on Mr. Kjær's new turbine were whooshing and whirring in the wind! "Hold on to your hats!" cried Søren Hermansen.

35   News travels fast on a small island like Samsø. After that night, everyone was asking how they could make energy of their own.

36   Suddenly, Søren Hermansen was busier than ever, helping people start new energy projects. The whole island got to work. Some people had big ideas. Some people had small ones. But all of them were important in working toward our goal.

37   The Holm family installed solar panels on their farm. Today their sheep are munching grass while the panels soak up energy from the sun.

38   Ingvar Jørgensen built a biomass furnace. It burns straw instead of oil, and now heats his house and his neighbors' houses, too.

39   In fact, biomass is so big on Samsø that whole villages are now heated by burning wood and straw grown on the island.

40   Erik Andersen makes tractor fuel oil from his canola crop.

41   And Brian Kjær's wife, Betina, whizzes around in an electric car. Their windmill powers the batteries.

42   Today we even have electric bicycles, charged by the power of the wind.

Wind Energy

Windmills were first invented over 1,000 years ago in the land that is now Iran. Back then the windmills were used to grind corn and pump water.

Windmills are still used in the modern world, and they can do lots more than grind corn. The wind turbine, a modern type of windmill, actually makes electric power.

When wind blows across a wind turbine's blade, the blade turns and causes the main shaft to spin a generator, which makes electric power. The more wind there is outside, the faster the blades turn, and the more energy the turbine makes.

Before a turbine is built, scientists take measurements to discover which places are the windiest. Today there are turbines on hills, on top of city buildings, and even in the ocean! The electricity that is created by wind turbines can be used to power a single home or building, or it can be connected to an energy grid where the electricity is shared by a whole community.

43   Every one of us has an energy independence story. And that's why people all over the world want to hear the latest news from Energy Island.

44   Let's see if Jørgen Tranberg will take us up the ladder to the very top of his fantastic wind turbine, so we can see what Samsø looks like today.

45   As you can see, there's plenty going on! Now we have lots of wind turbines. Down there is Samsø's brand new learning center, the Energy Academy, where kids and grownups from all over the world come to learn about what we've achieved, and to talk about new ideas for creating, sharing, and saving energy.

46   Guess who the director of the academy is. An extraordinary teacher named Søren Hermansen.

47   Things have certainly changed on our little island in the past few years.

48   We no longer need the oil tankers to bring us oil. And we don't need electricity from the mainland. In fact, on very windy days we have so much power that we send our own electricity back through the cable under the sea for other people in Denmark to use!

49   Samsø may be a small island, but we have made a difference in the world—reducing our carbon emissions by 140 percent in just ten years. And we did it by working together.

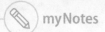

50 So that's how we got the name Energy Island!

51 And what can you do to make a difference on *your* island?

52 What's that? You say you don't live on an island?

53 Well, maybe you *think* you don't live on an island, but actually you *do*. We all do. We're all islanders on the biggest island of them all—planet Earth. So it's up to us to figure out how to save it.

54 There's renewable energy all around us. We just need to work together to make the best use of it. Hold on to your hats!

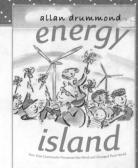
Respond to the Text

Collaborative Discussion

Look back at page 144. Tell a partner what you learned. Then work with a group to discuss the questions below. Use details from *Energy Island* to support your ideas. Take notes and use them to respond.

1. Review pages 150–153. What evidence shows that the children of Samsø are more excited about the energy project than the grownups?

2. Compare the way the people of Samsø used energy at the beginning of *Energy Island* with how they met their energy goals after the storm. What changed?

3. Review pages 160–162. How does the author show that the island is a good example for others? What evidence shows that others share the author's point of view?

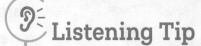

Listening Tip

If you can't hear someone in your group easily, ask that person to speak a little louder.

Speaking Tip

Say your ideas clearly and at a pace that isn't too fast or too slow.

Write an Encyclopedia Entry

In *Energy Island*, you learned how a community worked together to change the way they used energy. The people started using renewable resources to power their island.

Imagine that an online encyclopedia has asked readers to create a new entry about renewable resources and you want to submit an entry. Write a paragraph about renewable energy resources using information you learned from *Energy Island*. Think about the positives and negatives of renewable resources. Don't forget to use some of the Critical Vocabulary words in your writing.

Write facts and details about renewable resources you find in the text and in the sidebars.

WRITE

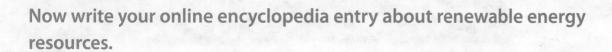

Now write your online encyclopedia entry about renewable energy resources.

Make sure your encyclopedia entry
☐ states your central idea clearly.
☐ is organized in a logical way.
☐ includes facts and details about renewable energy resources.
☐ ends with a concluding sentence.

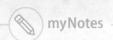
Notice &
Note
Aha Moment

Prepare to Read

GENRE STUDY **Historical fiction** is a story that is set in a real time and place in the past.

- Historical fiction might include real people as characters and fictional, or made-up, characters.
- Historical fiction includes characters who act, think, and speak like real people from the past would.
- Authors of historical fiction tell the story through important events.

SET A PURPOSE **Look at** the illustrations and story title. What would you like to learn about the storyteller and her candle? Write your ideas below.

Meet the Author and Illustrator:
Lucía González and Lulu Delacre

CRITICAL VOCABULARY

slender

gallant

chimed

preparations

flickered

concluded

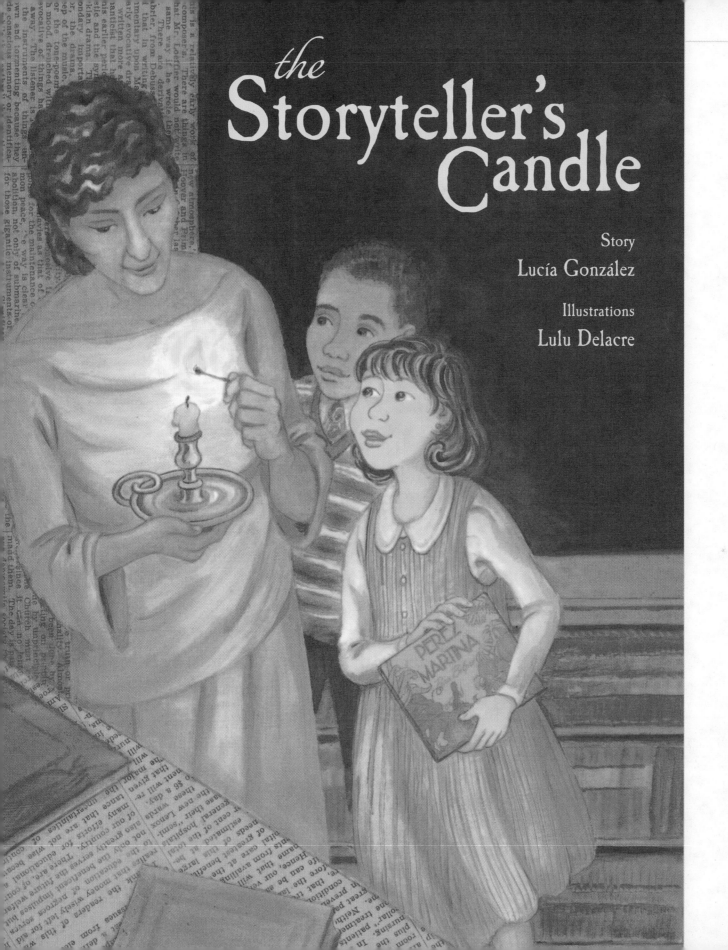

the Storyteller's Candle

Story
Lucía González

Illustrations
Lulu Delacre

INTRODUCTION

1   During the early years of the Great Depression (1929–1935), many Puerto Ricans left their little island to find work and better opportunities in the big city, *Nueva York*. Most lived in a section of northern Manhattan that became known as *El Barrio*, which means "the neighborhood" in Spanish.

2   Winter was harsh for the people of *El Barrio*. This was when they most missed their island's tropical warmth. But during this time something wonderful happened. A talented storyteller named Pura Belpré was hired to work as the first Puerto Rican librarian in the New York Public Library system. Through her work, her stories, and her books, Pura Belpré brought the warmth and beauty of Puerto Rico to the children of *El Barrio*.

—*Lucía González*

3   Hildamar shivered with cold as she walked home from school with her cousin Santiago. The icy afternoon wind froze their hands and burned their faces. It was the last week of school before winter break. It was also Hildamar's first *Navidad* in New York!

4   The winter surprised Hildamar. She had never felt so cold before! Only a few months earlier, Hildamar had traveled with her family from Puerto Rico to New York on a large ship called *El Ponce*. The journey took five days. Now the summer sun seemed very far from *El Barrio*.

5   And so Hildamar and Santiago rushed home as fast as they could to warm their hands by the old iron stove.

6   That evening, the family sat down to eat together.

7   "*Bendito!*" Mamá Nenita said with a sigh. "How I miss the soft breeze of December nights on our little island!"

8   "Ahh!" said Tío Pedro, Santiago's father. "I miss the delicious *pasteles* and the smell of roasting pork everywhere!"

9   "I remember the *parrandas* and *aguinaldos*, when family and neighbors came to visit, sing, dance, and eat!" said Titi María, Santiago's mother, closing her eyes and humming.

10 "*El Dia de los Reyes*, Three Kings' Day, was the best day of the year!" Santiago chimed in.

11 "Do the Kings travel this far?" asked Hildamar. "Will they come this year?"

12　The next day, like every day on their way to school, Hildamar, Santiago, and Titi María passed a tall building with windows that seemed to invite them inside. This building was different from the dark apartment buildings that stretched from one street corner to the other.

13　"Titi María, what's inside?" Hildamar asked. "Can we go in?"

14　"That's the library," Titi María replied, "and libraries are not for noisy *niños* like you."

15　"How about grown-ups like you?" asked Santiago.

16　"We don't speak English, and the people in there don't speak Spanish," she told them. And so it was that they never went inside.

17 But then, that afternoon, a special guest came to Hildamar and Santiago's class. She was a tall, slender woman with dark eyes that sparkled like *luceros* in the night sky. When she spoke, her hands moved through the air like the wings of a bird.

18 "*Buenos días*, good morning," she said. "My name is Pura Belpré. I come from the public library, and I bring stories and puppets to share with you today."

19 Ms. Belpré told stories with puppets, in English and in *español*. Everyone laughed at the story of silly Juan Bobo chasing a three-legged pot. At the end of her show, Ms. Belpré invited the children to visit the library during winter vacation.

20 "The library is for everyone, *la bíblioteca es para todos*," she said.

21 Hildamar couldn't wait to tell everyone in *El Barrio* the good news.

22 When Titi María picked the children up from school that day, they told her about the special guest, the stories, the puppets, and the library.

23 "Titi! Titi! They speak Spanish at the library!" Hildamar shouted.

24 "Can we go to the library today?" Santiago begged.

"*Español?* In the library? But *nenes*, I am very busy today," she explained. "I promise I'll take you one day."

25 "I want *mami* to come, too," said Hildamar, "but she's always working."

26 "Maybe we can all go on Saturday," suggested Titi María.

27 "*Viva!* Hurray!" Hildamar and Santiago clapped and skipped all the way to the *Bodega Santurce*, where Don Ramón and Doña Sofía sold *habichuelas*, fresh vegetables, bread, and *café*.

slender If something is slender, it is thin.

28   "And why are these *nenes* so happy today?" asked Doña Sofía, leaning from behind the countertop.

29   "Tell us, what's the good news?" asked Don Ramón.

30   "Don Ramón, they speak Spanish at the library!" declared Hildamar. The other customers in the store were very interested in what Hildamar had to say.

31   "*Qué bueno!*" they exclaimed.

32   "Do they have books in Spanish, too?" Doña Sofía wanted to know.

33   "*Bueno, ya veremos*—we'll see," said Don Ramón.

34   That Saturday, Hildamar's mother and Titi María invited Doña Sofía and Don Ramón to come with them to the library. Santiago invited his best friend Manuel.

35   The group walked along the snow-covered sidewalks, remembering *Navidades* back home. Soon they arrived at the handsome building.

36   The adults stopped to look up at the tall doors, doubting whether they should go inside. Hildamar, Santiago, and Manuel ran up the stairs, leaving them behind. They couldn't wait!

37 Inside, children filled the story room. Ms. Belpré welcomed them with a smile. "*Bienvenidos!* Welcome!" she said.

38 The storyteller's candle was lit and soon the story began. "*Había una vez y dos son tres en Puerto Rico . . .* Once upon a time in Puerto Rico . . ." Ms. Belpré told a story that Hildamar and Santiago had heard from their grandmother, about a beautiful Spanish cockroach named Martina and a gallant little mouse, Ratoncito Pérez. The story ended with a wave of applause.

39 "Now, close your eyes and make a wish," whispered Ms. Belpré. "We'll blow out the storyteller's candle and your wish will come true."

40 The children closed their eyes tight and wished.

41 When the children opened their eyes, Ms. Belpré made a special announcement. "*El Dia de los Reyes,* Three Kings' Day, is coming. This year we want to have a big *fiesta* at the library, with a play, dances, and a parade. The play will be the story of Pérez and Martina. Who wants to be in the play?"

42 Santiago raised his hand. "I want to help!" he called.

43 "I want to help, too!" the others chimed in.

44 Santiago was chosen to be Ratoncito Pérez. Hildamar raised her hand. Her heart was beating fast when Ms. Belpré picked her to play the most important part— Cucarachita Martina.

45 "We have the cast of characters," said Ms. Belpré, "but we will also need costumes, music, and a stage."

> **gallant** If you are gallant, you are thoughtful and very brave.
> **chimed** If you chimed in, you said something to agree with what someone else said.

46   Soon, word got around: "They speak Spanish at the library! And there's going to be a *fiesta* for Three Kings' Day there!"

47   Doña Sofía told Don Ramón, who told Padre Simón, who made an announcement at church. That Sunday, after morning mass, the *vecinos* gathered together. Even Pura Belpré attended the meeting.

48   "For the first time," they said, "*El Dia de los Reyes* will be celebrated in New York!"

49   Everyone wanted to help.

50   "I'll make the costumes," said Titi María.

51   "I'll make the curtains for the stage," said Mamá Nenita, who worked in a sewing factory.

52   "And I'll make the stage," said Don Ramón. "I was a carpenter in Puerto Rico."

53   From that day on, the neighbors went to the library every day to help with the preparations for the big event. They were very happy to discover books and magazines for them in *español* on the shelves.

54   The children rehearsed the play, the dances, and the stories. Don Ramón donated boxes and crates from his *bodega* to make the decorations. The mothers from *El Barrio* met at church or the library to paint, cut, and paste.

55   Finally, by the evening of January 5th, the library was ready for Three Kings' Day.

> **preparations** The things that have to be done to get ready for an event are preparations.

56   The next day, everyone came from far and near. Outside, the snow was rising high. Inside the library, the logs burned in an open fireplace and the storyteller's candle flickered. The room bubbled with the voices of children and adults. Everyone spoke at once, in Spanish and in English.

57   "Ay, *qué lindo!* How beautiful!"

58   The reading room had become an island in the Caribbean. A group of children sang *aguinaldos* while others waited impatiently for the show.

> **flickered**   If a flame flickered, it gave off a light that moved in an unsteady way.

59   "¡A*salto!*" boomed the voices of the *parranderos*,
surprising everyone. The children stretched up on tiptoe for
a good look.

60   "*Saludos, saludos, vengo a saludar . . .*" sang the *parranderos*.

61   Doña Sofía shook the *maracas, chiki-chiki-chik, chiki-chik.*
Don Ramón scraped the *güiro, cha-kra-cha-kra-cha.* And
leading the group, strumming the *cuatro*, was Señor Lebrón.

62   Suddenly, there they were—the Three Kings! They
marched through the room sprinkling the children
with candies and sweets.

63   The music stopped, and the play began. "Many
years ago, in a little round house with a little round
balcony, there once lived a Spanish cockroach
named Martina . . ."

64   Hildamar stepped on stage. She was the
most beautiful cockroach! And Santiago . . .
ay, what a handsome little mouse!

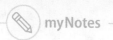

65 Ms. Belpré concluded the show in her usual way. "Close your eyes and make a wish," she whispered as she held the storyteller's candle.

66 Hildamar closed her eyes and wished. When she opened them, her eyes met Ms. Belpré's. With her gentle smile and twinkling eyes, Ms. Belpré said, "Today, with everyone's help, we brought the warmth and beauty of Puerto Rico to New York. Remember, the library belongs to you all. We'll blow out the storyteller's candle, and your wish will come true."

concluded When you have concluded something, you have ended it.

Respond to the Text

Collaborative Discussion

Look back to page 166. Tell a partner what you learned. Then work with a group to discuss the questions below. Refer to details from *The Storyteller's Candle* to support your ideas. Come to the discussion prepared to join in the conversation.

1. Review page 170. What does the text tell you about how the family feels about life in New York?

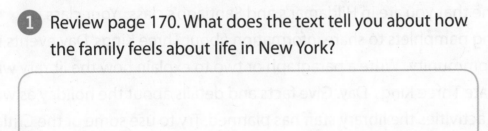

2. Reread pages 176–181. How do Hildamar, Santiago, and the people of their community feel about the story about the Spanish cockroach, Martina, and the mouse, Ratoncito Pérez? What details in the text support this?

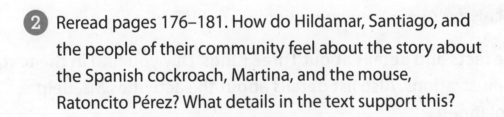

3. What details in the text show that Three Kings' Day is important to the Puerto Rican people?

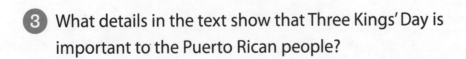

 **Listening Tip**

Listen to hear the exact details the speaker uses to answer a question. What is another example you can add?

Speaking Tip

Restate an idea you agree with and suggest an idea to build on what was said.

Write a Pamphlet

In *The Storyteller's Candle*, you read about how Hildamar and Santiago discover the library in their new city is a wonderful place. You also read about Ms. Belpré's plans for the Three Kings' Day celebration.

Imagine that you are in Hildamar's and Santiago's class. Your class is creating pamphlets to share information about Three Kings' Day events in your community. Write a paragraph or two to explain how the library will celebrate Three Kings' Day. Give facts and details about the holiday as well as the activities the library staff has planned. Try to use some of the Critical Vocabulary words in your writing.

Write facts and details about Three Kings' Day you find in the text and illustrations. Also list details about the activities Ms. Belpré has planned.

WRITE ....

Now write your pamphlet about Three Kings' Day.

✓

Make sure your pamphlet
☐ begins by introducing your topic.
☐ tells facts and details about the holiday.
☐ tells about the activities the library has planned.
☐ provides a conclusion encouraging people to participate.

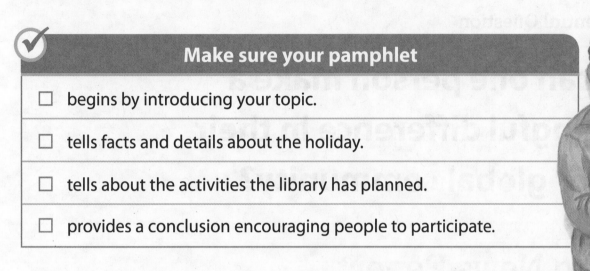

Essential Question

How can one person make a meaningful difference in their local or global community?

Write a News Report

PROMPT Think about what you learned about how people can make an impact in their communities from the selections in this module.

Imagine that you are writing a report for your school newspaper. Explain how people can impact their communities. Use text evidence from the selections to provide examples of these important people.

I will write about _____.

Make sure your news report
☐ includes an introduction that explains the topic.
☐ is organized into paragraphs based on your supporting details.
☐ uses text evidence and includes transition words to connect ideas.
☐ ends with a strong conclusion.

Look back at the selections and review the notes you took. Which ideas help you explain the topic?

In the chart below, write a central idea for your report. Then use evidence from the texts to write supporting details. Include facts and examples from the texts to expand on your supporting details. Try to use Big Idea Words and Critical Vocabulary in your writing.

My Topic: _____

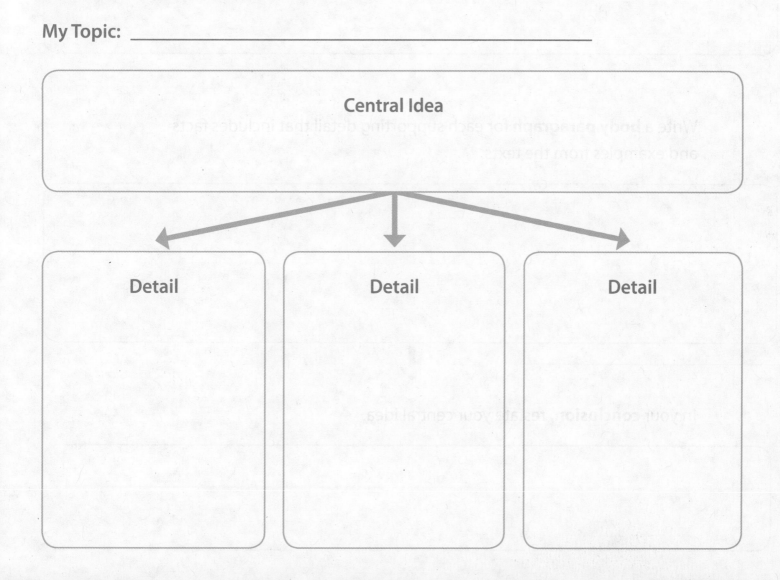

Central Idea

Detail

Detail

Detail

DRAFT ·· **Write your report.**

Use the information you wrote on page 187 to draft your report. Write an
introduction that grabs readers' attention and states your central idea.

Write a **body paragraph** for each supporting detail that includes facts
and examples from the texts.

In your **conclusion,** restate your central idea.

The revision and editing steps give you a chance to look carefully at your writing and make changes. Work with a partner to determine whether you have explained your ideas clearly to readers. Use these questions to help you evaluate and improve your report.

PURPOSE/ FOCUS	ORGANIZATION	EVIDENCE	LANGUAGE/ VOCABULARY	CONVENTIONS
☐ Does my report state a clear central idea? ☐ Have I stayed on topic?	☐ Does my introduction get my audience's attention? ☐ Have I provided a strong conclusion?	☐ Does the text evidence I've included support my ideas?	☐ Did I use linking words to show connections and help my ideas flow smoothly? ☐ Did I use descriptive words?	☐ Have I spelled all the words correctly? ☐ Have I used verbs and adverbs correctly?

PUBLISH ···················· Share your work.

Create a Finished Copy Make a final copy of your news report. You may want to include photos or illustrations. Consider these options to share your report:

1. Create a slideshow presentation, and share it with a small group.

2. Publish your report with others as part of a classroom newsletter. Have classmates take it home for family and friends to read.

3. Share your report with the class as part of a news broadcast.

Imagine! Invent!

"To invent, you need a good imagination and a pile of junk."

—Thomas Edison

What does it take to make a successful invention?

Get Curious
Video

Words About Inventors and Inventions

The words in the chart below will help you talk and write about the selections in this module. Which words about inventors and inventions have you seen before? Which words are new to you?

Add to the Vocabulary Network on page 193 by writing synonyms, antonyms, and related words and phrases for each word.

After you read each selection in this module, come back to the Vocabulary Network and keep building it. Add more ovals if you need to.

WORD	MEANING	CONTEXT SENTENCE
invention (noun)	An invention is something created by a person that did not exist before.	The invention of the telephone changed the way people communicate.
brilliant (adjective)	When a person, idea, or thing is brilliant, it is extremely clever or skillful.	Benjamin Franklin was a brilliant genius when it came to his experiments with electricity.
productive (adjective)	If you are productive, you are able to do a lot with the time and resources that you have.	The most productive student will finish his daily tasks and more in a regular school day.
original (adjective)	Something described as original is the first of its kind.	My grandparents own an original record player from the early 1900s.

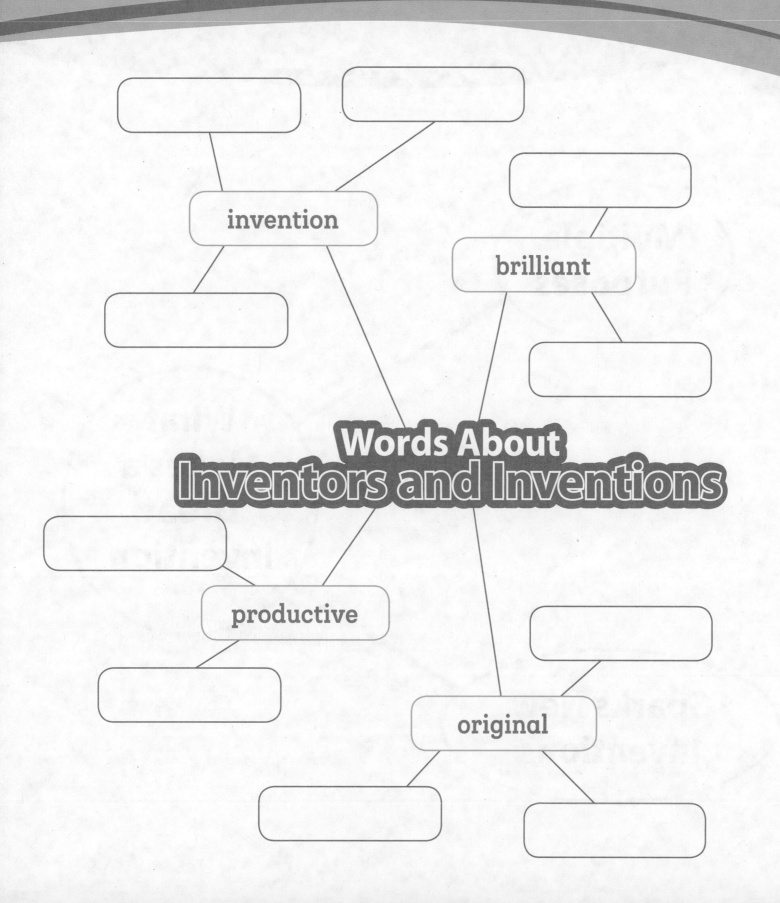

invention

brilliant

Words About
Inventors and Inventions

productive

original

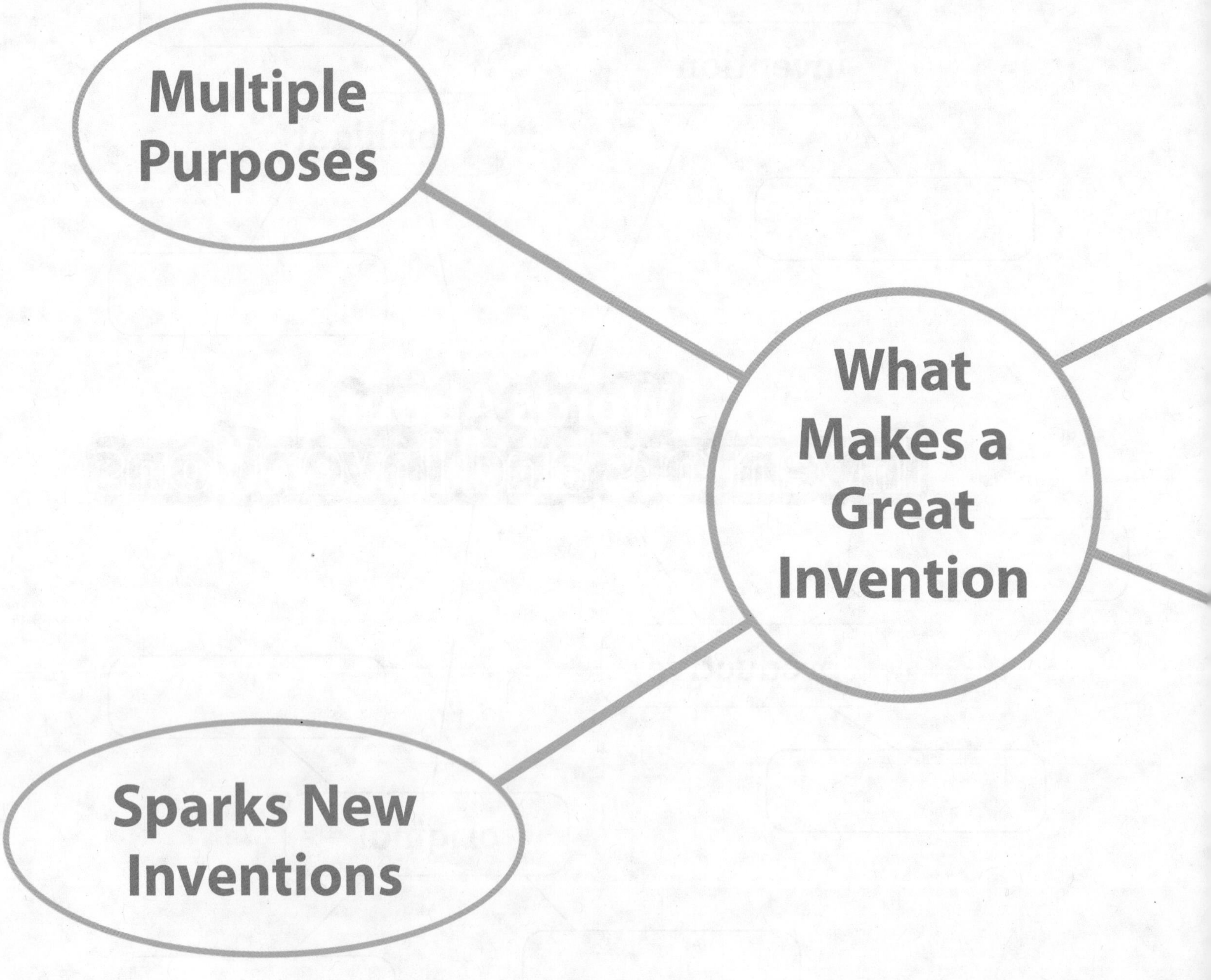

Multiple Purposes

What Makes a Great Invention

Sparks New Inventions

Original Idea

Solves a Problem

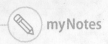
A Century *of* Amazing Inventions

1   It starts with an "Aha!" moment. An inventor has a brilliant idea. Then he or she creates something that never existed before. An invention can be a device, a process, or a discovery. Often it solves a problem and makes life easier. Sometimes it just makes life more fun.

2   During the 20th century (1900–1999), inventors were bursting with original ideas. Many of their inventions are part of daily life today. The timeline on the next page shows some of the 20th century's most memorable inventions.

1900

1903

AIRPLANE

Brothers Orville and Wilbur Wright owned a bicycle shop. That's not how they became famous, though. They invented one of the first airplanes, which helped make people's dreams of flying come true.

TELEVISION

Philo Farnsworth grew up in a home without electricity, yet at age 21, he invented the television. In his lifetime, the productive Farnsworth invented hundreds of other things as well.

1928

BUBBLEGUM

For centuries, people chewed the gum, or sap, from trees. Walter Diemer came up with an idea for making stretchier gum. His invention keeps kids popping bubbles to this day.

SKATEBOARD

1958

No one knows who first thought of attaching roller-skate wheels to a board, but it was probably a surfer. Surfing was becoming more and more popular in the late 1950s, and skate-boarding became a way to "surf" on the street.

VIDEO GAME

The first video game was called *Tennis for Two*. It was invented at Brookhaven National Laboratory in New York. A lighted dot acted like a tennis ball. Players "hit" the ball back and forth by pushing a button.

1977

PERSONAL COMPUTER

CELL PHONE

1983

One of the earliest personal computers had a keyboard but no screen. To use it, people connected it to a television.

The cell phone had been around for 10 years before anyone could buy one. One of the first cell phones weighed nearly two pounds and cost almost $4,000!

2000

Prepare to Read

GENRE STUDY A **biography** is the story of a real person's life written by someone other than that person.

- Authors of biographies may organize their ideas using headings and subheadings.
- Biographies often include photographs or illustrations from the person's life.
- Biographies include third-person pronouns such as *he, she, him, her, his, hers, they, them,* and *their.*

SET A PURPOSE **Think about** the title and the genre of this text. What do you already know about Thomas Edison? What do you think you will learn about him and his inventions? Write your ideas below.

CRITICAL VOCABULARY

valuable

device

breakthrough

dictation

technology

radar

**Meet the Author and Illustrator:
Gene Barretta**

Timeless Thomas

How Thomas Edison Changed Our Lives

GENE BARRETTA

1 *Have you ever* thought about inventing something of your own? You're never too young to try.

2 Thomas Alva Edison began experimenting when he was just a boy. That's right. It was the beginning of a life dedicated to improving the world with his brilliant ideas and inventions.

3 But Thomas couldn't do it alone. When he grew up, he gathered a large team of scientists, engineers, mechanics, and artisans in Menlo Park, New Jersey. Together, they started the first research and development laboratory in the world. It became known as the Invention Factory.

Laboratory pipe organ

Menlo Park Laboratory

Pet bear cub

4 Later, a second lab was built in West Orange, New Jersey. It was even bigger and busier. These were the sites of his greatest successes and his most valuable failures. Edison used his failures as a necessary part of inventing. He once said, "I know several thousand things that won't work." And he would always try again.

valuable   If something is valuable, it is useful, helpful, or important.

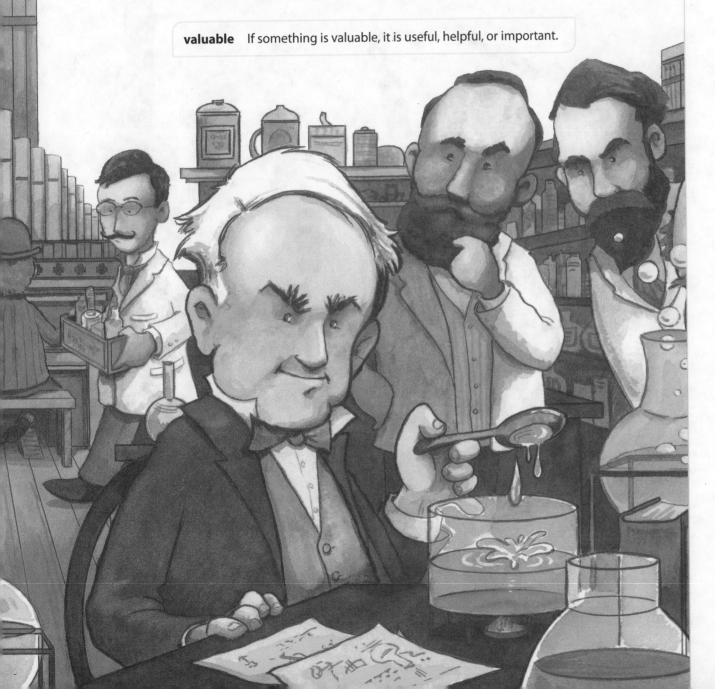

Present Day

5   We can now record any sound we like and save it. This was not possible before Edison.

Edison's Lab

6   Edison's tinfoil phonograph was the first device to record sound and play it back. It was a major scientific breakthrough and earned him his nickname, The Wizard of Menlo Park. That's pretty impressive for a man who was partially deaf.

To record:
Cover the cylinder with tin. Rotate it and speak into the horn.

To listen:
Stop and place the needle back to the start. Rotate the cylinder.

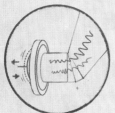

The voice vibrates a needle on the end of the horn.

The needle rides over the sound grooves and plays your recording.

The vibrating needle makes small sound grooves on the rotating tin.

device   A device is a tool or machine that has a certain purpose.
breakthrough   If you make a breakthrough, you make an important discovery after many tries.

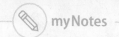
Present Day

7   If Thomas Edison were alive today, he would be fascinated by the many ways we listen to recorded sounds. It all started with his phonograph.

Edison's Lab

8   Edison constantly improved on his phonograph so it could have multiple purposes. Models were designed for homes and public arcades.

9   Phonographs were also introduced to offices as the first dictation machines. It became possible for office workers to record spoken information, save it, then play it back when they were ready to copy it down.

10   A small phonograph was built for the first talking doll.

---

dictation   The word *dictation* describes the act of writing down words that have been spoken.

Present Day

11   Need a battery? Take your pick. Today they are made in many shapes and sizes.

Edison's Lab

12   One of Edison's biggest successes was his nickel-iron storage battery. It was originally created to power an electric car. But since the electric car didn't catch on, he found many other important uses for it.

13   For example, Edison's battery was used to power:

Buoys

Boats and submarines

Local delivery trucks

Railway cars and signals

Rural homes

Miners' lamps

Present Day

→

14   When members of our government cast a vote, they use very basic voting machines.

→

16   The X-ray machine is a common way to photograph the inside of our bodies.

Edison's Lab

15   Thomas Edison invented a vote recorder for the government. It was his very first patent. Having a patent means you legally own an invention. Over the course of his career, he was awarded 1,093 patents for his ideas.

17   Edison's fluoroscope was the first example of X-ray technology. It generated bright and fast images. The basic design is still used today.

> **technology**   Technology is the use of science to invent useful things or to solve problems.

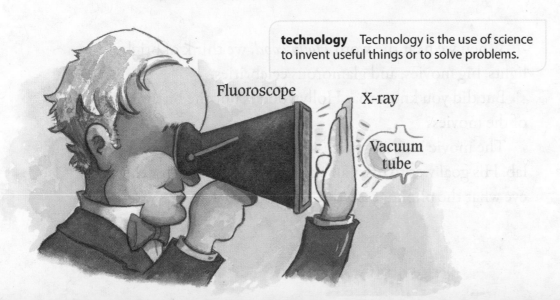

Fluoroscope   X-ray

Vacuum tube

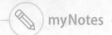
Present Day

18   When we hear the word *Hollywood*, we think of bright lights, big movies, and glamorous celebrities.

19   But did you know that Hollywood is not the birthplace of the movies?

20   The movie industry was essentially started at Edison's lab. His goal was to offer an experience that "does for the eye what the phonograph does for the ear."

Edison's Lab

21   So Edison created the first motion picture camera, the Kinetograph. The technology was similar to our modern movie cameras. He also built the first movie studio and called it the Black Maria because it resembled a police patrol wagon with the same nickname.

22   Movie lights did not exist yet. So they opened the roof and used the sunlight. As the sun moved, the studio followed it on a revolving track.

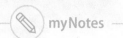
Present Day

23   Today we can watch our favorite movies on a big screen, at home, or even on our phones.

Edison's Lab

24   The first movies were shown on Edison's Kinetoscope, which did not project images onto a screen. It was built for peephole viewing—one person watched at a time.

25   Edison's Kinetophone was the first projector to show movies with synchronized sound. The projector was connected to a phonograph. It wasn't perfect, but it was the first.

26   When people watched movies for the first time, they were amazed to see even the simplest movements, like . . .

| a woman dancing | a man sneezing | a boat in the water | a man posing | a rooster walking |

Present Day

27   When you chat with your friend on a computer, you send electronic messages across wires and radio waves, just like the old telegraph machines did. Edison began working as a telegraph operator in his teens.

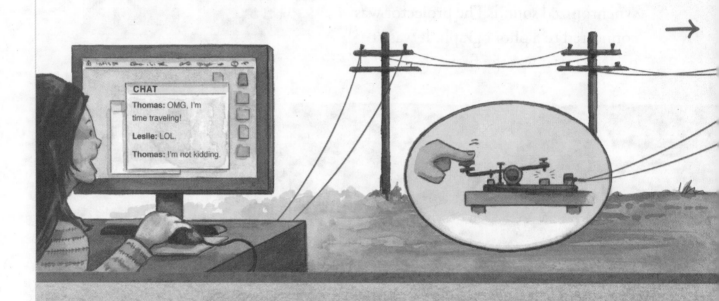

CHAT

Thomas: OMG, I'm time traveling!

Leslie: LOL.

Thomas: I'm not kidding.

29   Today we use radio waves to transmit all types of signals, including those from mobile phones, radar, television, and radio.

radar   Radar is a way to find unseen objects by using radio signals.

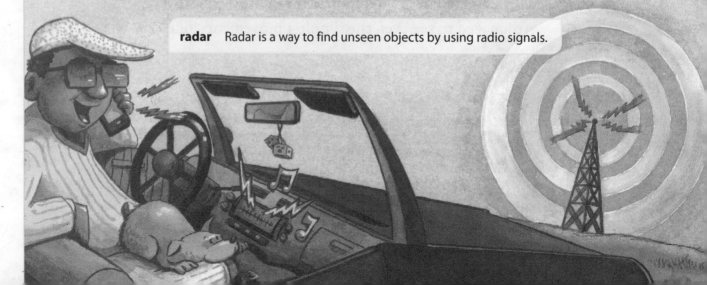

Edison's Lab

28   He eventually improved telegraph technology with machines that could not only send messages faster, but could also send several different messages on the same wire and in opposite directions.

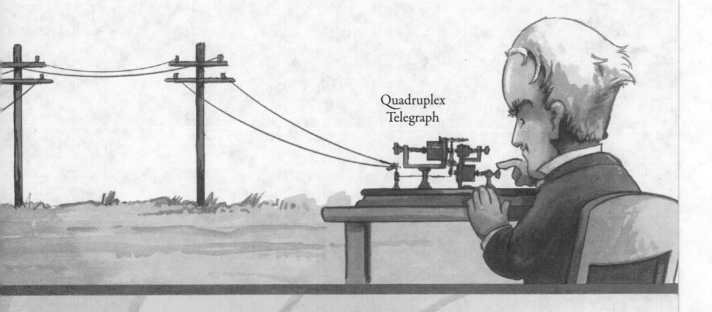

Quadruplex
Telegraph

30   Thomas Edison was among the first to discover radio waves in the air, although at the time, he couldn't fully explain his discovery.

Present Day

31   Our quality of life has certainly been improved by the extraordinary work of Thomas Edison and his colleagues at the labs. Think about this: bedtime stories would be very different today if it were not for Edison's most popular and important invention, the incandescent lightbulb.

Edison's Lab

32   After thousands of experiments, Thomas Edison produced a lightbulb that was perfect for homes and offices. It was sturdy, safe, and bright. It also burned a long time. This breakthrough ultimately changed the way we live. And it was also excellent for shadow puppets.

Present Day

33   Edison's bulb worked as part of an elaborate light and power system large enough to power an entire city. He once told a newspaper that he would be the first person to light up a portion of New York City. It took four years of hard work, but he kept his word.

Edison's Lab

34   Edison built the first large electric generator and power system on Pearl Street in Manhattan. The key feature was its ability to send electricity to many different locations at once. It became the model for the future.

PEARL STREET STATION

MAIN

35 So every time you turn on a light, think of Thomas Edison and remember everything he gave us.

36 One of the greatest tributes to his work came on the day of his funeral in 1931. President Herbert Hoover asked the entire country to honor Edison by turning off the lights for a minute of darkness.

37 People everywhere honored a lifelong career filled with important inventions and innovations—a career that began in the small home laboratory of a young boy with lots of ambition and dreams.

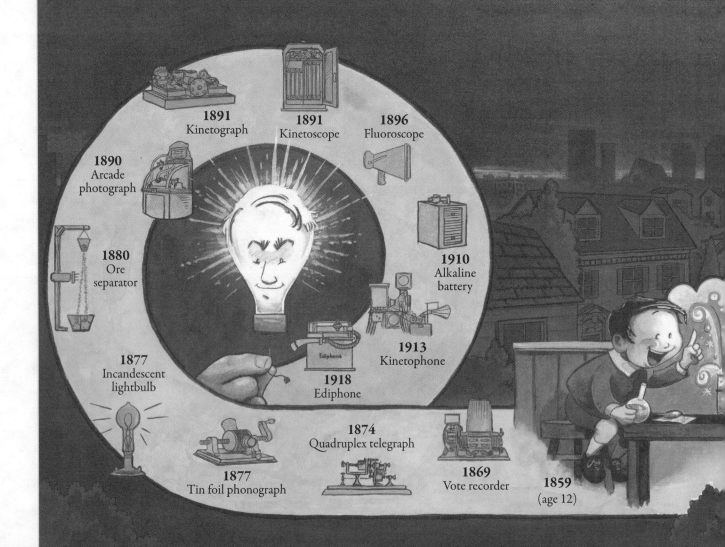

1891 Kinetograph

1891 Kinetoscope

1896 Fluoroscope

1890 Arcade photograph

1880 Ore separator

1910 Alkaline battery

1877 Incandescent lightbulb

1918 Ediphone

1913 Kinetophone

1874 Quadruplex telegraph

1877 Tin foil phonograph

1869 Vote recorder

1859 (age 12)

Respond to the Text

Collaborative Discussion

Look back at what you wrote on page 198. With a partner discuss your ideas about Thomas Edison and his inventions. Then work with a group to discuss the questions below. Refer to details in *Timeless Thomas* to support your ideas. Take notes for your responses.

1. Reread page 203. Why did Edison think his failures were important?

2. Review pages 206–207. What are some reasons that Edison's phonograph was a useful invention?

3. What details in the text explain why the whole country wanted to honor Edison on the day of his funeral?

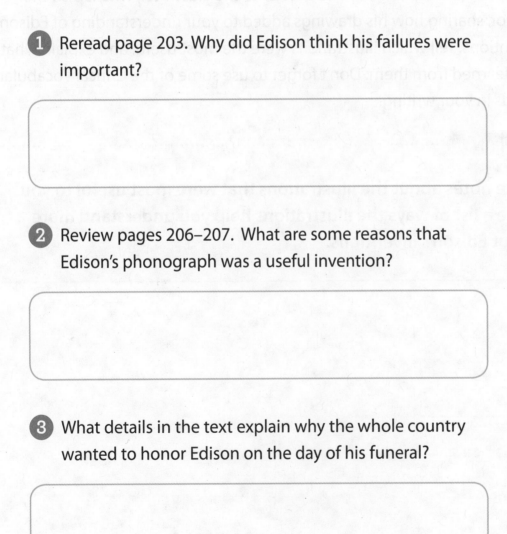

Listening Tip

Listen carefully when a group member asks you a question. What information is the speaker asking for?

Speaking Tip

When a group member asks you a question, first restate his or her question to make sure you understand what he or she is asking.

Write a Friendly Letter

PROMPT ....

In *Timeless Thomas*, you learned how our quality of life is better in many ways because of Thomas Edison's inventions. The text and the illustrations work together to share information about Edison's ideas.

Study the pictures. Then write a letter to the illustrator, who is also the author, sharing how his drawings added to your understanding of Edison's inventions. Tell which illustrations were the most useful and explain what you learned from them. Don't forget to use some of the Critical Vocabulary words in your writing.

PLAN ....

Make notes about the illustrations that were most useful to you. Write a list of ways the illustrations help you understand more about Edison's inventions.

WRITE

Now write your letter to the illustrator.

Make sure your letter
☐ begins with a greeting and ends with a closing.
☐ states your opinion about the illustrations and provides reasons to support your opinion.
☐ shows extra information you learned about Edison's inventions.
☐ uses linking words like *because, since,* and *for example*.

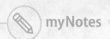

**Notice &
Note**
Word Gaps

Prepare to Read

GENRE STUDY **Informational texts** give facts and examples about a topic.

- Authors of informational texts may present their ideas in sequential, or chronological, order.

- Authors of informational texts may organize their ideas by stating a problem and explaining its solution and/or explaining causes and effects.

- Informational texts include visuals, such as illustrations and timelines.

SET A PURPOSE **Think about** the title and genre of this text, and look at the images. What do you know about bicycles? What would you like to learn about how they have changed over the years? Write your responses below.

**Build Background:
Bicycle Racing**

**CRITICAL
VOCABULARY**

contraption

quest

craze

era

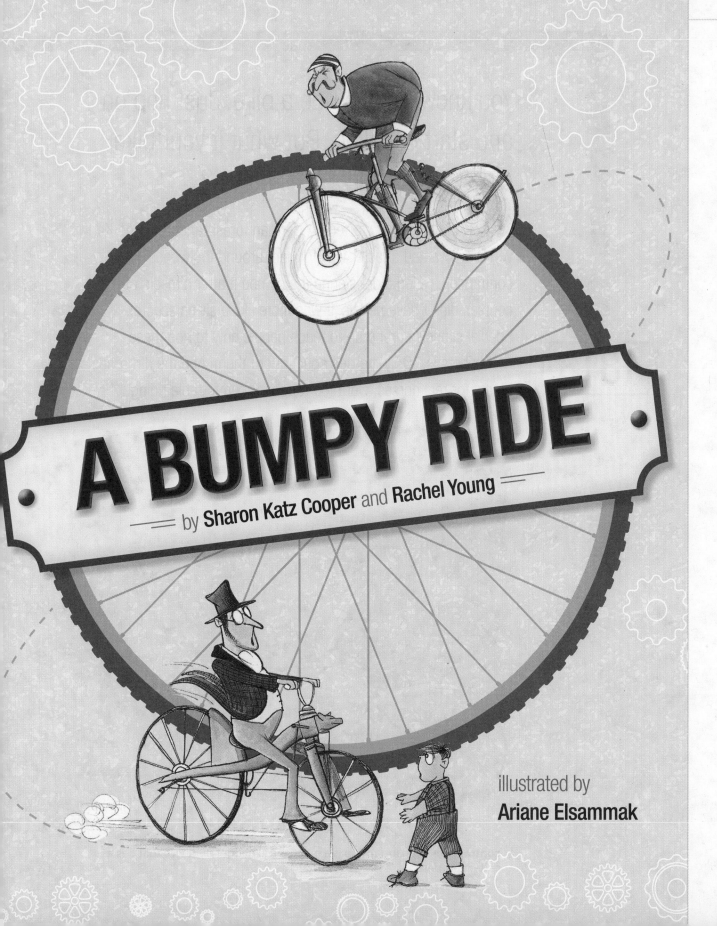

A BUMPY RIDE

by **Sharon Katz Cooper** and **Rachel Young**

illustrated by
Ariane Elsammak

1   You know how to ride a bike. Just hop on and start pedaling. But what if your bike didn't have pedals? Or brakes?

2   How did bikes get started? A German forest ranger named Karl von Drais wanted a faster way to roam around the woods. His contraption, called a draisienne (he named it after himself, of course), didn't have pedals. It was more like a sit-on scooter. Special schools sprang up to teach people how to ride these "hobbyhorses." Only the rich could afford them. And the dirt roads, meant for real horses, were too rough for comfortable riding.

> **contraption**   A contraption is a mechanical gadget or device that has a certain purpose.

·1821·

3   The hobbyhorse needed more oomph, but people didn't believe you could balance on two wheels without your feet touching the ground. One solution was a hobbyhorse with a handlebar you pulled to make the front wheel spin faster. These awkward machines were not a hit with anyone but mail carriers. They used them for deliveries.

4   Kirkpatrick Macmillan, a Scottish blacksmith, built the first real bicycle. It had foot pedals that turned the back wheel. It reached top speeds of 14 miles (23 km) per hour, but the pedal-powered bike was hard to steer. Macmillan caused the first bike wreck when he plowed into a crowd of people and knocked down a small child.

·1839·

·1861·

5   A French carriage maker named Pierre Michaux moved the foot pedals to the front wheel. This made the "hobbyhorses" easier to ride, and more people began to try them out. They were even used in carousels at fairs. But with hard metal tires, the machines earned their nickname, "boneshakers."

·1870·

6   Since the pedals were directly attached to the bicycle's front wheel, each time the pedal went around once, the wheel went around once. So to go faster, you needed a bigger wheel (more distance for each pedal). Front wheels got bigger and bigger until they were 5 feet (1.5 m) across. To save weight, the back wheel shrank. The fast, big-wheeled bikes became so popular that they were called "ordinaries." Getting on one was a little out of the ordinary, though. You had to have a boost from a friend or a running start and then hope that the road ahead was smooth. Bumps sent riders flying over the handlebars, which was known as "taking a header."

·1881·

7   Ordinaries were popular with adventurous young men, but older riders wanted a safer machine. They stuck to quadricycles and tricycles. Queen Victoria of England bought two trikes. They didn't have brakes, but who needs brakes when you're only going walking speed?

·1885·

8   In a quest to make two-wheelers safer, along came the Rover, the first "safety" bike. It worked a lot like the one you ride today. Pedals turned a chain. The chain turned the rear wheel. A larger gear ring in front and a small one in back meant that each push of the pedal turned the rear wheel several times. So the wheel didn't need to be huge. The new bicycles were fast, safe, and less expensive, but with their solid rubber tires, the ride was still pretty bumpy.

quest   If you go on a quest, you go in search of something important to you.

10   With safe, cheap, comfortable bikes, cycling became a national craze. Cycling clubs sprang up all over. Bicycle races were popular, especially 100-mile "centuries." Cyclists also pushed to get roads paved—dirt, gravel, and mud are hard on bikes. Doctors even worried about the possible effects of riding too much. The strain of balancing, for instance, might cause "bicycle face."

11   Women, youth, and working people particularly enjoyed the new freedom bikes gave them. Before bikes, only rich people with horses could go out and see the country. Now, anyone could go. It's hard to ride in long skirts, so many women cyclists started wearing puffy pants known as "bloomers." This started a fashion revolution that finally ended the era of long dresses for good.

9   To give his son a more comfortable ride, John Boyd Dunlop wrapped a garden hose around the wheels of his tricycle. Water-filled hoses didn't work very well, but air-filled hoses were a success. The modern tire was born.

·1889·

·1890s·

craze   If there is craze for something, it is very popular for a period of time.

era   An era is a period of time in history.

·1975·

12   In the early days of cycling, many riders were hurt by pitching over the handlebars. A few wore leather caps, which didn't do much to cushion the blow. But when biking got popular again in the 1970s, riders demanded good helmets that actually protected the head. Finally!

·THE FUTURE?·

1896 SAFETY BIKE

13   Although bikes keep getting stronger and faster, the basic bike shape hasn't changed much in the last 100 years. It's a simple, efficient design that's hard to improve on. Today in the United States, we get around mostly by car, but bikes are still the most popular vehicles on Earth. Who knows? Maybe someday they'll rule the roads again.

MODERN BIKE

Collaborative Discussion

Look back at what you wrote on page 226. With a partner discuss your ideas about what you learned. Then work with a group to discuss the questions below. Refer to details in *A Bumpy Ride* to support your ideas. Take notes for your responses.

1. Reread page 230. What feature did Kilpatrick Macmillan add to make the first real bicycle? What were some problems with it?

2. Review pages 232–233. Why did bicycles change from the "ordinaries" of 1870 to the Rover in 1885?

3. What details in the text explain how bicycles became very popular in the 1890s?

Listening Tip

As you listen, think about how you can add to the discussion. Plan what you want to say about each question.

Speaking Tip

If you would like more information, ask group members questions to help you understand their ideas.

Write a Magazine Article

....

Before you read *A Bumpy Ride*, did you know that a bicycle was first called a "hobbyhorse"? Do you think you could ride a bicycle with a tire that is five feet wide?

Imagine you are a writer for *Bicycling Today* magazine. Your editor has asked you to write a brief article about bicycles of the past. Using the facts and details in *A Bumpy Ride*, write an article that describes the major developments in the history of the bicycle and the problem each development solved.

PLAN ....

Make a list of the most important milestones in the history of the bicycle. Write down the year of the milestone and a short summary of how bicycles changed that year.

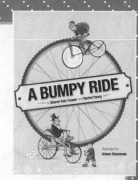

WRITE

Now write your magazine article about bicycles of the past.

Make sure your magazine article

- ☐ introduces the topic.

- ☐ includes facts and details from the text.

- ☐ tells about events in the order they occurred.

- ☐ describes how each development solved a problem with the previous design.

- ☐ features words about bicycles that are used in the text.

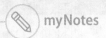

Notice & Note
Words of the Wiser

Prepare to Read

GENRE STUDY **Narrative poetry** tells a story using a poetic structure.

- Narrative poetry tells a story through the plot—the main events of the story.
- Narrative poems include sound effects to reinforce the meaning of the poem.
- Narrative poems often include word sounds, such as alliteration and onomatopoeia, to emphasize particular words or ideas.

SET A PURPOSE **Think about** the title and genre of the text, and look at the illustrations. What story do you think this narrative poem will tell? Write your ideas below.

CRITICAL VOCABULARY

engineer

perplexed

dynamo

lingers

whirled

baffled

**Meet the Author and Illustrator:
Andrea Beaty and David Roberts**

ROSIE REVERE, ENGINEER

by **Andrea Beaty** illustrated by **David Roberts**

1 THIS IS THE STORY OF ROSIE REVERE,
who dreamed of becoming a great engineer.
In Lila Greer's classroom at Blue River Creek,
young Rosie sat shyly, not daring to speak.

2 But when no one saw her, she peeked in the trash
for treasures to add to her engineer's stash.
And late, late at night, Rosie rolled up her sleeves
and built in her hideaway under the eaves.

engineer   An engineer is a person who
uses science to design and build machines.

3   Alone in her attic, the moon high above,
    dear Rosie made gadgets and gizmos she loved.
    And when she grew sleepy, she hid her machines
    far under the bed, where they'd never be seen.

4   When Rosie was young, she had not been so shy.
    She worked with her hair swooping over one eye
    and made fine inventions for uncles and aunts:
    a hot dog dispenser and helium pants.

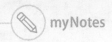
5 The uncle she loved most was Zookeeper Fred.
She made him a hat (to keep snakes off his head)
from parts of a fan and some cheddar cheese spray—
which everyone knows keeps the pythons away.

6. And when it was finished, young Rosie was proud,
but Fred slapped his knee and he chuckled out loud.
He laughed till he wheezed and his eyes filled with tears,
all to the horror of Rosie Revere,
who stood there embarrassed, perplexed, and dismayed.
She looked at the cheese hat and then looked away.
"I love it," Fred hooted. "Oh, truly I do."
But Rosie Revere knew that could not be true.
She stuck the cheese hat on the back of her shelf
and after that day kept her dreams to herself.

> **perplexed** If you are perplexed, you feel confused and worried about something.

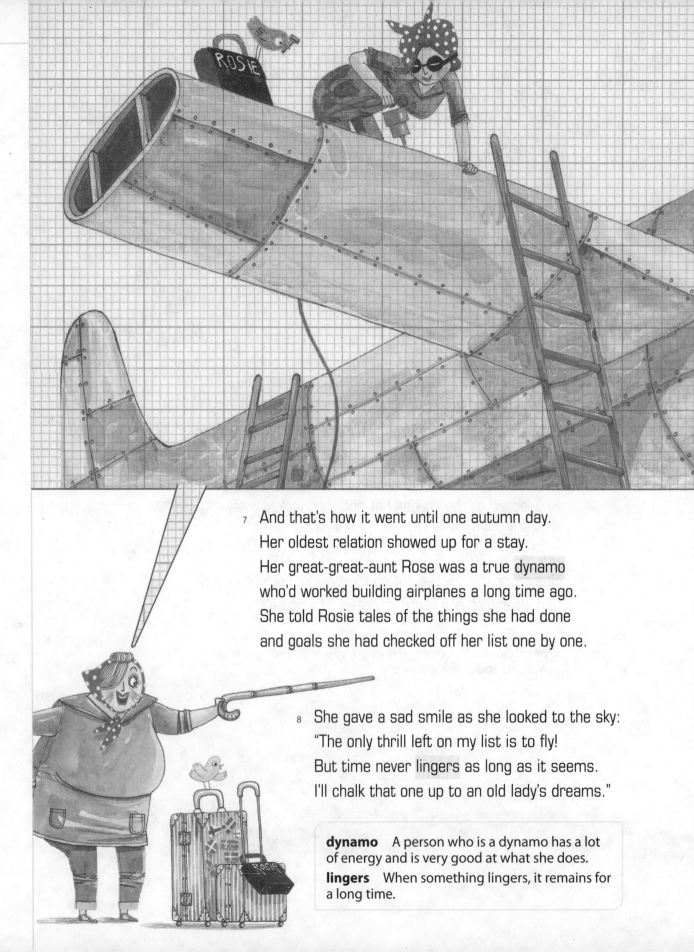

7 And that's how it went until one autumn day.
   Her oldest relation showed up for a stay.
   Her great-great-aunt Rose was a true dynamo
   who'd worked building airplanes a long time ago.
   She told Rosie tales of the things she had done
   and goals she had checked off her list one by one.

8 She gave a sad smile as she looked to the sky:
   "The only thrill left on my list is to fly!
   But time never lingers as long as it seems.
   I'll chalk that one up to an old lady's dreams."

> **dynamo**   A person who is a dynamo has a lot
> of energy and is very good at what she does.
> **lingers**   When something lingers, it remains for
> a long time.

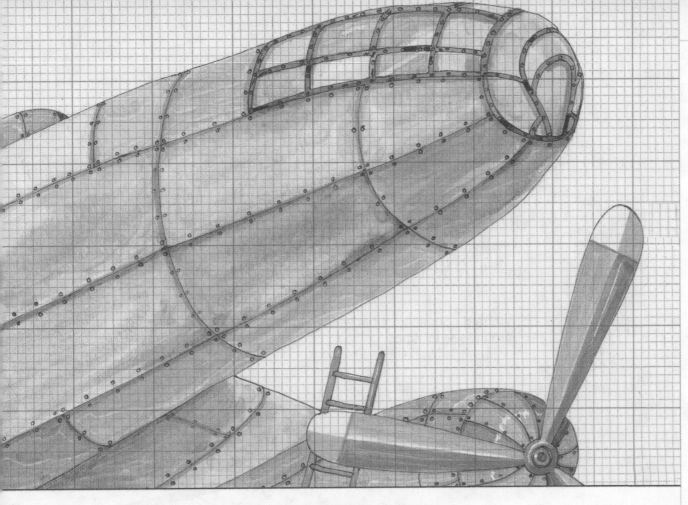

9 That night, as Rosie lay wide-eyed in bed,
a daring idea crept into her head.
Could *she* build a gizmo to help her aunt fly?
She looked at the cheese hat and said, "No, not I."

10 But questions are tricky, and some hold on tight,
and this one kept Rosie awake through the night.
So when dawn approached and red streaks lit the sky,
young Rosie knew just how to make her aunt fly.

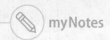

11 She worked and she worked till the day was half gone,
then hauled her cheese-copter out onto the lawn
to give her invention a test just to see
the ridiculous flop it might turn out to be.

12 Strapped into the cockpit, she flipped on the switch.
The heli-o-cheese-copter sputtered and twitched.
It floated a moment and whirled round and round,
then froze for a heartbeat and crashed to the ground.

> **whirled**   Something that whirled turned
> around several times.

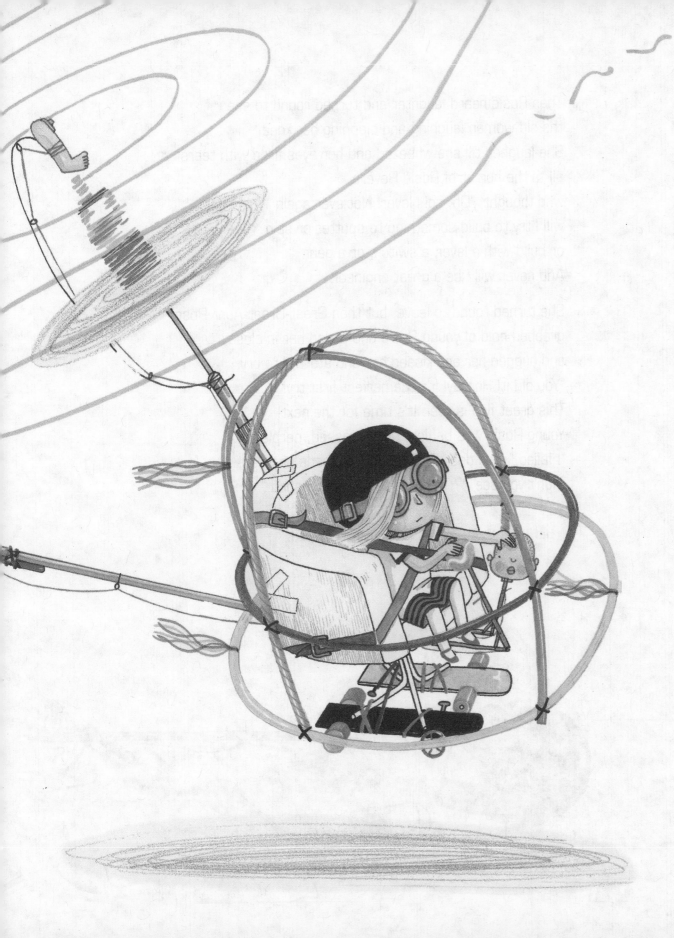

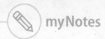

13 Then Rosie heard laughter and turned round to see
the old woman laughing and slapping her knee.
She laughed till she wheezed and her eyes filled with tears
all to the horror of Rosie Revere,
who thought, "Oh, no! Never! Not ever again
will I try to build something to sputter or spin
or build with a lever, a switch, or a gear.
And never will I be a great engineer."

14 She turned round to leave, but then Great-Great-Aunt Rose
grabbed hold of young Rosie and pulled her in close
and hugged her and kissed her and started to cry.
"You did it! Hooray! It's the perfect first try!
This great flop is over. It's time for the next!"
Young Rosie was baffled, embarrassed, perplexed.
"I failed," said dear Rosie. "It's just made of trash.
Didn't you see it? The cheese-copter crashed."

baffled If you are baffled, you are confused.

250

"Yes!" said her great aunt. "It crashed. That is true.
But first it did just what it needed to do.
Before it crashed, Rosie . . .
before that . . .
it flew!"

15 "Your brilliant first flop was a raging success!
Come on, let's get busy and on to the next!"
She handed a notebook to Rosie Revere,
who smiled at her aunt as it all became clear.
Life might have its failures, but this was *not* it.
The only true failure can come if you quit.

16 They worked till the sun sneaked away to its bed.
Aunt Rose tied her headscarf around Rosie's head
and sent her to sleep with a smile ear-to-ear
to dream the bold dreams of a great engineer.

17 At Blue River Creek all the kids in grade two
build gizmos and gadgets and doohickeys too.
With each perfect failure, they all stand and cheer,
but none quite as proudly as Rosie Revere.

Collaborative Discussion

Look back at what you wrote on page 240. With a partner discuss your ideas about the story. Then work with a group to discuss the questions below. Refer to details in *Rosie Revere, Engineer* to support your ideas. Take notes for your responses, and use your notes to ask and answer questions.

1 Reread pages 242–243. What details in the text show that Rosie does not want to share her inventions and ideas?

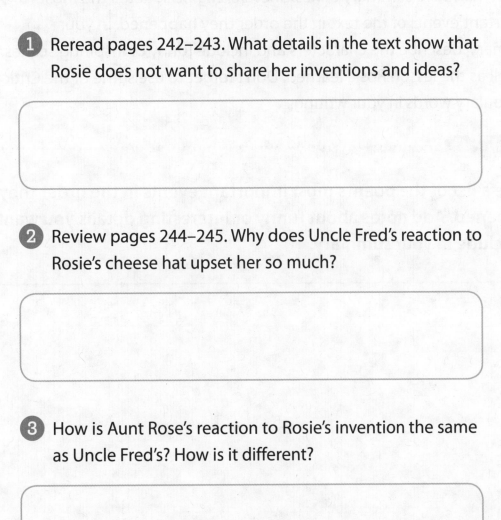

2 Review pages 244–245. Why does Uncle Fred's reaction to Rosie's cheese hat upset her so much?

3 How is Aunt Rose's reaction to Rosie's invention the same as Uncle Fred's? How is it different?

Write a Summary

Rosie Revere, Engineer tells the story of a young girl who wants to become an engineer. The funny and inspiring story is told through a rhyming poem that almost sounds like a song.

Write a narrative summary of *Rosie Revere, Engineer*. Retell the most important events of the text in the order they happened. In your summary, describe the characters and include funny or inspiring scenes, as well as the lesson Rosie learned. Don't forget to use some of the Critical Vocabulary words in your writing.

PLAN ···

Make a list of the poem's most important events in the order they happened. Add notes about funny or interesting details you want to include in your summary.

WRITE

Now write your narrative summary of *Rosie Revere, Engineer*.

Make sure your summary

- [ ] retells the story and is organized in the order events occurred.

- [ ] describes the major characters.

- [ ] tells what lesson Rosie learned.

- [ ] uses words like *first*, *next*, *then*, and *after* to show the event order.

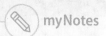
Prepare to Read

GENRE STUDY An **opinion text** gives an author's opinion about a topic and tries to convince readers to believe that opinion.

- Opinion texts often include first-person pronouns.
- Opinion texts include evidence, such as facts and examples, to support the author's viewpoint.
- Authors of an opinion text may organize their ideas by making a comparison to a similar argument.

SET A PURPOSE **Think about** the title of this text. Look at the photographs. Which invention do you think the author believes is Edison's best invention? Write your ideas.

CRITICAL VOCABULARY

visionary

compact

singles

memorable

system

innovative

Build Background: Edison "Fun Facts"

EDISON'S BEST INVENTION

Thomas Edison was America's greatest inventor.

A true visionary, he invented so many things that we could argue about which one is his best invention! Some of Edison's most popular inventions are the kinetograph [kuh-NEET-uh-graf], the phonograph, and the light bulb, but in my opinion, Edison's best invention is the light bulb.

2   We can compare inventions in two ways. First, good inventions give people ideas that lead to new inventions. We can tell how good an invention is by looking at how many other inventions it has inspired. Second, good inventions change the way we live. Imagine the world without certain inventions. What would life be like? A truly good invention changes our lives for the better.

3   The light bulb has inspired the most new inventions, and it has made the biggest difference in our lives. But don't just take my word for it. Let's learn more about these three inventions, and then you can decide for yourself!

> **visionary**   A visionary is a person who has new or unusual ideas about life in the future.

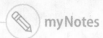

Kinetograph

4   According to Gene Barretta in *Timeless Thomas*, the kinetograph was "the world's first motion picture camera." The kinetograph inspired many more inventions. This inspiration led Edison to construct the first movie studio, the Black Maria. "Black Maria" was another name for the vans that the police of the time used to carry prisoners to jail. Edison's studio was small, stuffy, and had black walls—just like the police vans. So the workers called it the Black Maria. He also invented the kinetoscope and the kinetophone to show the first movies. The kinetoscope was a machine that allowed people to watch movies. The kinetophone was a kinetograph with a phonograph added to play sound along with the movie. Mr. Barretta says that the movie industry "essentially started at Edison's lab."

5   The kinetograph inspired people to invent new ways of recording life in motion. From TV cameras to cell phones, any invention that can record moving pictures was inspired by Thomas Edison's kinetograph. Inventors also created new ways to watch movies, such as television and online video sites.

6   Edison's kinetograph changed how we see the world. Today, you can watch all kinds of movies at a movie theater. You can choose from hundreds of TV channels and millions of videos on the Internet. You can also make your own movies with a cell phone!

You can watch recordings of past events as if you were right there. And you can watch live events, even if you can't be there in person.

7   Imagine a world without the invention of the kinetograph. Instead of watching movies and TV, you would go to plays and listen to storytellers. There would be no visual record of historical events. You would only read about them in books. It would be a very different world. The kinetograph made a huge change to our lives. That is why it is one of Edison's best inventions.

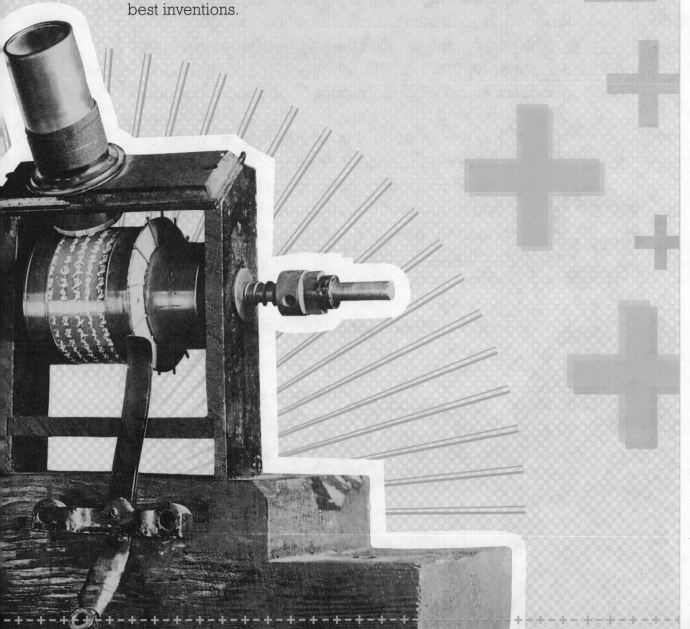

Phonograph

8   Gene Barretta writes that Edison's phonograph "was the first device to record sound and play it back." Mr. Barretta says it "was a major scientific breakthrough." The phonograph led to many more inventions. Edison invented the jukebox, the talking doll, and the dictation machine. Inventors who were inspired by the phonograph gave us vinyl records, compact discs, and digital music. Just as the movie industry started at Edison's lab, so did the music industry.

9   The phonograph changed the way we listen to music. Mr. Barretta writes that before Edison it "was not possible . . . to record any sound we like." Imagine a world without recorded sound! There would be no singles, albums, or music videos. The only way you would be able to listen to music would be to hear a live performance of a singer or musician. Since we would not be able to record people speaking, there would be no voicemail, audiobooks, or recordings of memorable speeches. Today, we can only imagine what the Gettysburg Address sounded like when Abraham Lincoln delivered it. But, because of the phonograph, we know exactly what Dr. Martin Luther King, Jr.'s "I Have a Dream" speech sounded like.

compact   Things that are compact can fit in a small space.

singles   Music singles are recordings of one song.

memorable   When something is memorable, it is special enough that people want to remember it.

Light Bulb

10   Gene Barretta says the light bulb is "Edison's most popular and important invention." Light bulbs are used in many other inventions, such as flashlights, automobile headlights, and electric signs. The light bulb inspired more than just new ways to shine light. Mr. Barretta writes that the light bulb "worked as part of an elaborate light and power system, large enough to power an entire city." Edison built the first example of this system on Pearl Street in New York City. This system was able "to send electricity to many different locations at once." It led to the power grids that carry electricity to customers around the country today.

11   Edison's innovative grid brought electricity into homes across America. The grid was built to power electric light bulbs. However, once people had electricity in their homes, they could use it to power other inventions. People came up with all kinds of electrical inventions—refrigerators, washing machines, and computers. The list goes on and on. If it were not for Edison's lightbulb, we would not have power grids today. Without power grids, we would not have inventions that run on electrical power.

system   A system is a set of things or ideas that work together to get something done.

innovative   An innovative idea is one that has never been thought of before.

12   The light bulb changed the world so much that it is hard to think of life without it. Before Edison, people used candles, oil lamps, or gas lights to make light. You could not make light without burning fuel. Burning candles and oil lamps caused many deadly fires. According to Gene Barretta, Edison's light bulb was "sturdy, safe, and bright." It made light without burning. Homes are now safer thanks to the light bulb. They are also brighter. Oil lamps burn through fuel very quickly. People only lit oil lamps for as long as they needed them. Mr. Barretta says that light bulbs "burned for a long time," far longer than any lamp.

13   Before the light bulb, the streets of big cities were lit by gas lights. Smaller towns used oil lanterns. Some places had no lights at all! People had to carry lanterns if they wanted to go anywhere after dark. Many people just stayed inside at night instead.

14   In my opinion, Gene Barretta is right to say that the light bulb "changed how we live." It brought safe, bright, and long-lasting light to homes, offices, and factories. Today, we do not have to stop doing things just because it is dark. With floodlights, we can play sports and go to concerts at night. Streetlights, traffic lights, and automobile headlights make our roads much safer. The light bulb has made a huge difference to how we live. It is certainly Edison's best invention. Still not convinced? Let's look at some more facts . . .

DID YOU KNOW?

Edison used Greek roots to name many of his inventions. For example, the word *kinetograph* comes from two Greek roots: *kinetikos* [kuh-NET-eek-oss], the Greek word for movement, and *graphe* [graf-ay], the Greek word for writing.

Kinetoscope also has two Greek roots *kinetikos* and *skopos* [suh-KOH-poss], the Greek word for target. Kinetophone has the Greek roots *kinetikos* and *phone* [fuh-OH-nay], the Greek word for sound or voice.

Phonograph also has two Greek root. Can you tell what they are?

Notice how knowing the meaning of the Greek roots can help you figure out what the inventions do. You can use the same trick for a lot of words used in science. If you know what the roots are, you can break the word down and figure out what it means.

Lighting the Way

15   Let's compare the light bulb with the kinetograph and the phonograph. First, how many new inventions did each of them inspire? The kinetograph led to the invention of video cameras, movies, television, and online video. The phonograph led to the invention of the jukebox, the vinyl record, compact discs, and MP3 players. The light bulb inspired the invention of many kinds of electrical lights, as well as power grids, and nearly every invention that uses electricity. The kinetograph and the phonograph led to many inventions, but not as many as the light bulb did. That is one reason why the light bulb is the best invention.

16   Great inventions also change the way we live. The kinetograph inspired inventions that allow us to see things from long ago or far away. The phonograph inspired inventions that allow us to hear music from around the world. The light bulb changed how we live, work, and play. Thanks to the light bulb, we can do things now that were not possible in the past. Our lives are easier. Our homes are brighter. Our streets are safer. All because of the light bulb! The kinetograph changed the way we see the world. The phonograph changed the way we hear the world. But the light bulb changed the world. If you disagree, think about what happens when the power goes out. A power outage shows what life was like before the light bulb. It can be fun at first, but no one is sorry when the lights come on again. That is another reason why I believe the light bulb is Thomas Edison's best invention.

17   Gene Barretta writes about the "greatest tribute" to Edison's talent as an inventor. President Hoover "asked the country to honor Edison by turning off the lights for a minute of darkness." That minute of darkness reminded everyone just how much Edison's best invention had changed the world.

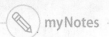
EDISON'S INVENTIONS

Inventions	What inventions did they inspire?	How did they change the world?
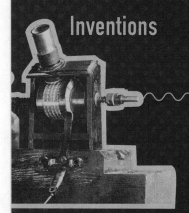 **kinetograph**	movie cameras, movie studios, movie theaters, kinetoscope, kinetograph, TV, online video	+ Allowed events to be recorded + Created the movie industry + Led to TV and online video
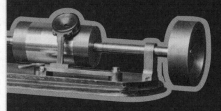 **phonograph**	jukebox, talking doll, dictation machine, microphone, vinyl records, compact discs, digital music, voicemail, audiobooks, answering machines	+ Allowed sounds to be recorded + Created the music industry + Led to music charts and pop stars
light bulb 	flashlights, automobile headlights, stadium floodlights, traffic lights, electric signs, power grids, many electrical inventions	+ Provided cheap, safe, long-lasting light in homes, offices, factories, and on city streets + Allowed people to travel, work, and play after dark + Drove the spread of power grids that send electricity to every home + Led to many inventions powered by electricity

Collaborative Discussion

EDISON'S BEST INVENTION

Look back at what you wrote on page 256. With a partner discuss your ideas about which invention the author thinks is best. Then work with a group to discuss the questions below. Refer to details in *Edison's Best Invention* to support your ideas. Take notes for your responses.

1 Reread page 259. What are the two ways the author compares inventions? What details show why the author chose those ways?

2 Review pages 260–261. Which new inventions came about because of Edison's kinetograph?

3 How were the kinetograph and the phonograph alike? How were they different?

Listening Tip

Listen carefully for each speaker's central idea. How would you restate that idea in your own words?

Speaking Tip

Help listeners notice your central idea. Use a complete sentence to state your idea.

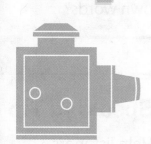

Write a Caption

PROMPT

In *Edison's Best Invention*, the author summarizes three of Thomas Edison's inventions. He includes facts and details to explain his choice for the best invention.

Imagine that you are creating a bulletin board or online display about inventions. The display will show photos or drawings of Edison's inventions, along with captions that give facts and details about them. The captions will also explain how the inventions changed the world and what other inventions they inspired. Using the chart on page 268, write a caption for the kinetograph, phonograph, or the light bulb. Don't forget to use some of the Critical Vocabulary words in your writing.

PLAN

Make notes about one of the inventions shown in the chart. List the most important details from the text, including what inventions were inspired by the invention you chose.

WRITE

Now write your caption for a bulletin board or online display about inventions.

✓ **Make sure your caption**

- ☐ introduces the invention.
- ☐ includes facts and details from the chart in the text.
- ☐ tells how the invention changed the world.
- ☐ explains how this invention inspired other inventions.
- ☐ uses linking words like *also, another, and,* or *more* to connect ideas.

? Essential Question

What does it take to make a successful invention?

Write an Opinion Essay

PROMPT Think about the inventors and inventions you read about in this module.

Imagine that a TV show called *The Next Great Inventor* has asked for students' ideas. They want to know what an inventor *most* needs to make a great discovery or gadget. Write an essay to share your opinion. Use examples and evidence from the texts to support your opinion.

I will write about _____.

✓ Make sure your opinion essay
☐ states your opinion.
☐ presents your reasons in a clear way.
☐ uses text evidence and examples as support.
☐ uses words such as *for example* to connect ideas.
☐ ends by reminding readers of your opinion.

PLAN .... **Gather information.**

What does a great inventor really need to have? Look back at your notes and review the texts to find support for your opinion.

Plan your essay by completing the chart below. Write a sentence that states your opinion. Then write your reasons and the details that support each one. Use Critical Vocabulary words where you can.

My Topic: ______________________________

My Opinion

Reason 1

Reason 2

Reason 3

Performance Task

Use the information you wrote on page 273 to draft your opinion essay.
Write an **introduction** that states your opinion. A clever start will make
readers want to find out more!

Write a **body paragraph** that gives your reasons and support. Use linking
words to connect ideas.

In your **conclusion**, remind readers of the one thing that great inventors need.

The revision and editing steps give you a chance to look carefully at your writing and make changes. Work with a partner to determine whether you have explained your ideas clearly to readers. Use these questions to help you evaluate and improve your opinion essay.

PURPOSE/ FOCUS	ORGANIZATION	EVIDENCE	LANGUAGE/ VOCABULARY	CONVENTIONS
☐ Do I state my opinion in a clear way? ☐ Do all of my reasons support my opinion?	☐ Do I show how reasons connect to my opinion? ☐ Does the ending restate my opinion?	☐ Did I include evidence from the texts?	☐ Did I use linking words to connect my opinion and reasons? ☐ Did I use exact words to explain my reasons?	☐ Does each sentence begin with a capital letter and have the correct end punctuation? ☐ Did I use possessive nouns correctly?

Create a Finished Copy Make a final copy of your opinion essay. You may want to include a photo or drawing. Consider these options to share your essay:

1. Include your essay in a classroom display about great inventors.

2. Present your essay to the class. Read it aloud and respond to questions from the audience.

3. Share your essay on a school website or social networking page. Ask for feedback from readers.

From Farm to Table

"My grandfather used to say that once in your life you need a doctor, a lawyer, a policeman . . . but every day, three times a day, you need a farmer."

— Brenda Schoepp

? Essential Question

How does food get to your table?

Get Curious
Video

Words About Getting Food from Farm to Table

The words in the chart below will help you talk and write about the selections in this module. Which words about farming and food have you seen before? Which words are new to you?

Add to the Vocabulary Network on page 279 by writing synonyms, antonyms, and related words and phrases for each word.

After you read each selection in this module, come back to the Vocabulary Network and keep building it. Add more ovals if you need to.

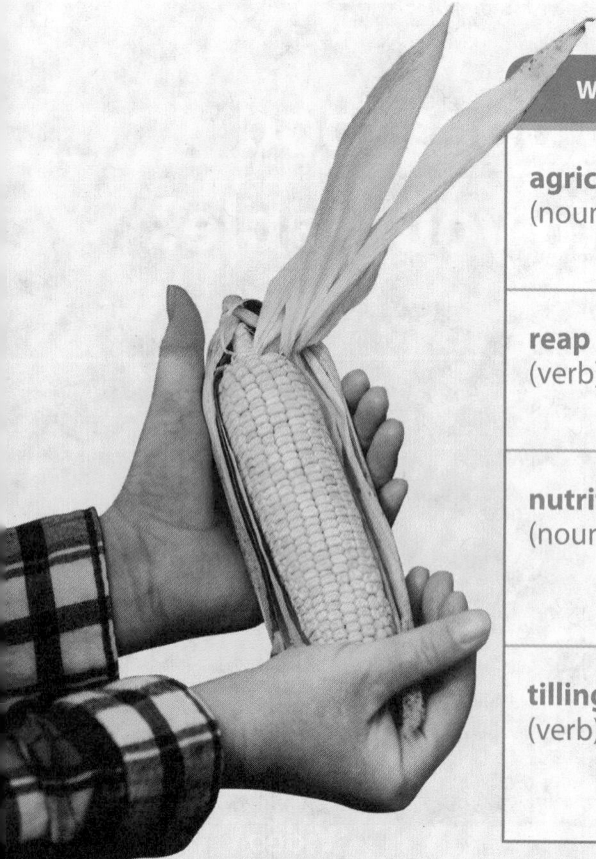

WORD	MEANING	CONTEXT SENTENCE
agriculture (noun)	Agriculture is the practice of farming, producing crops, and raising animals.	A tractor is used in agriculture to pull machinery that plows and plants crops.
reap (verb)	When you reap a crop, you cut and gather what you need from it.	The farmer will reap the corn when it is ready for harvest.
nutrition (noun)	Nutrition is the process of eating the right kinds of foods to be healthy.	I want to learn about good nutrition so that I will know which foods can keep me healthy.
tilling (verb)	If you are tilling the land, you are preparing the soil for farming and raising crops.	The farmer is tilling the land by turning over the dirt and getting it ready for planting the seeds.

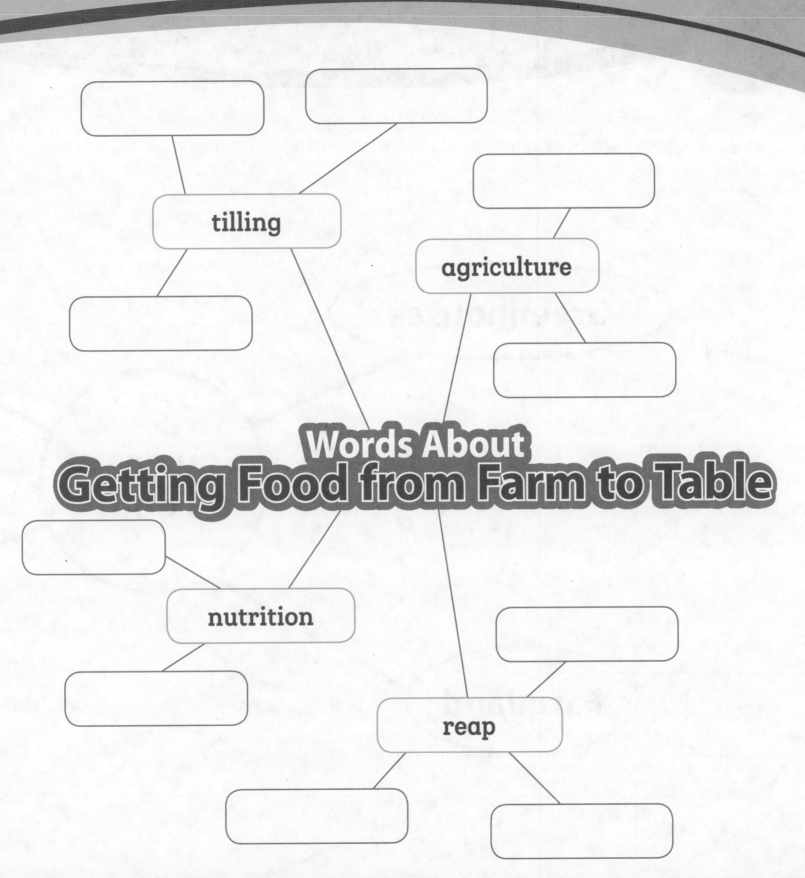

Words About
Getting Food from Farm to Table

tilling

agriculture

nutrition

reap

Knowledge Map

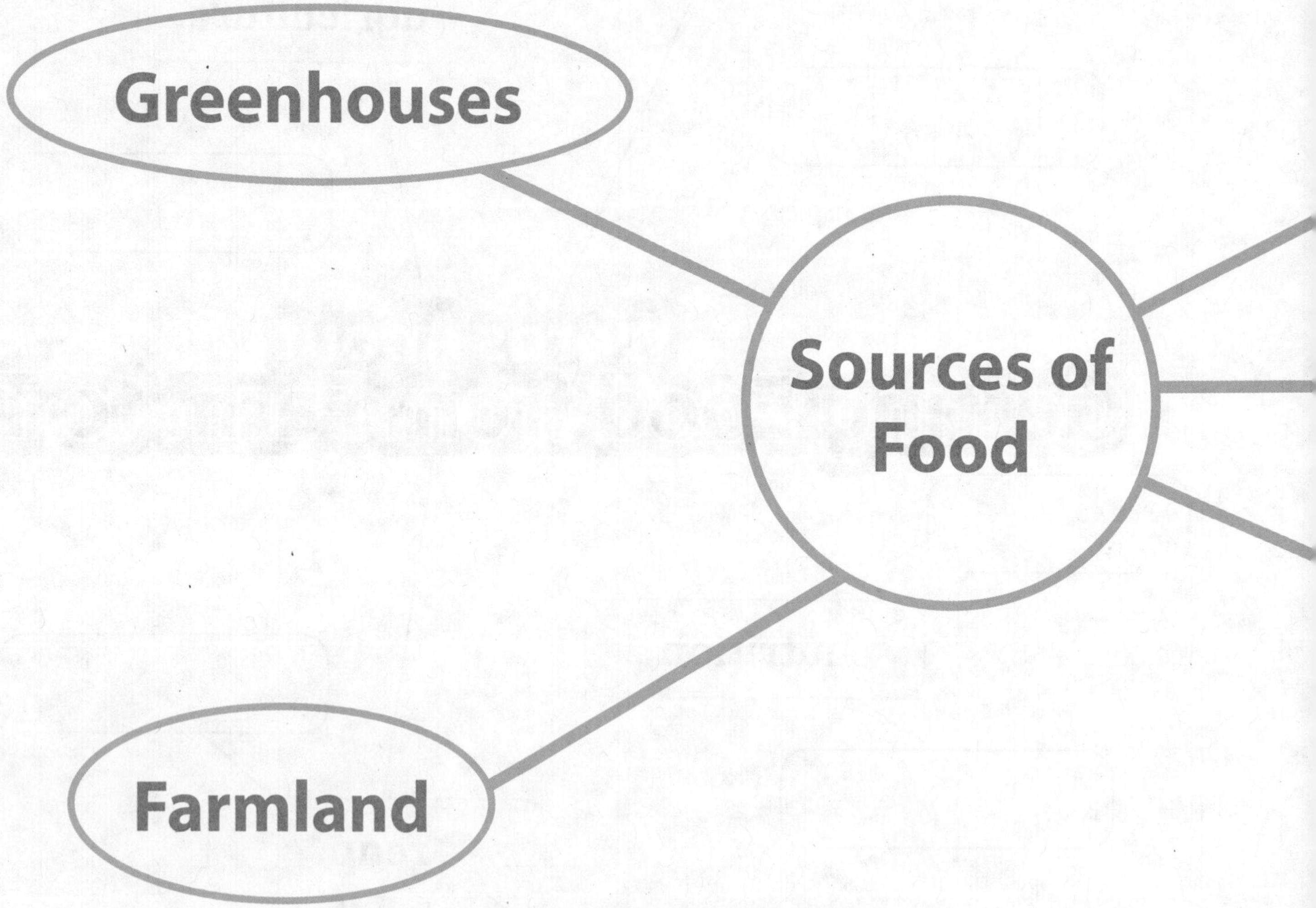
Greenhouses
Sources of Food
Farmland

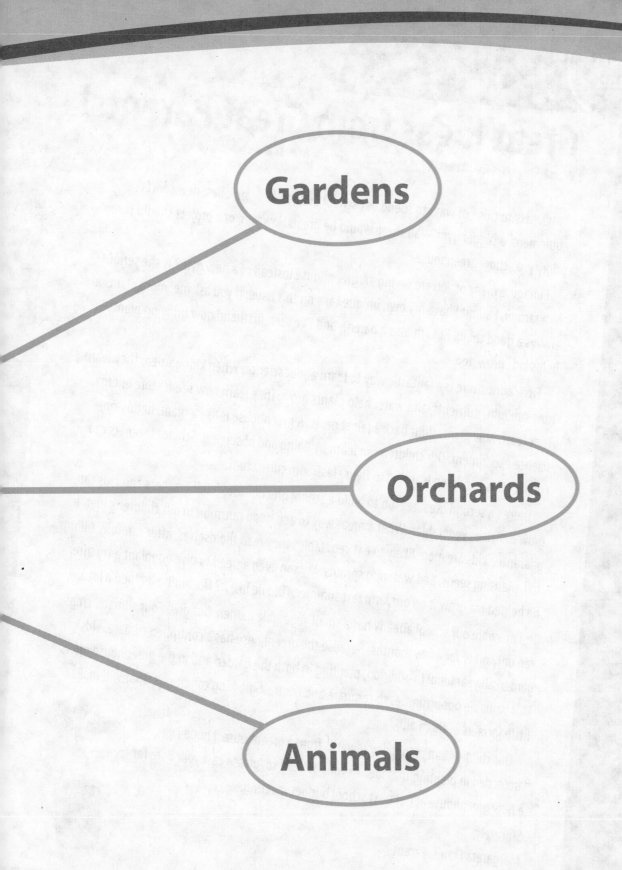

Gardens

Orchards

Animals

Short Read

Great Ideas from Great Parents!

Washington Elementary Needs a Greenhouse

1   It's easy to think of ways to spend our school budget. New supplies, new sports equipment, a bigger gym—all these would be great. However, one project should take priority: a school greenhouse.

2   I imagine many of you are saying, "A greenhouse instead of a new gym? Is she serious?" As a farmer, I admit I have my own unique take on this issue. If you ask me, more plants are always a good thing. But I'm also a parent, and I've seen firsthand how growing plants helps kids grow, too.

3   First, agriculture is a fantastic way to learn about science. When kids garden, they learn how sunlight, nutrients, and water help plants grow. They learn how seeds store energy. They learn how plants fight back against pests. A greenhouse is like a giant, hands-on science experiment. Our children can learn by doing and observing. Science teachers can connect this hands-on learning to their classroom curriculum.

4   There's a second great reason to build a school greenhouse: food! Teachers and kids can grow delicious vegetables. What a great way to add good nutrition to our children's diet. I guarantee kids are more likely to eat vegetables they reap themselves, after carefully tilling soil, planting seeds, and watering sprouts. My son even agreed to give eggplant a try after he helped me grow it on our farm last summer. (Did he like it? No, but he learned a lot.)

5   I'm aware our school already has a small vegetable garden, but given our climate, crops can only grow for a few months. Because the greenhouse has a controlled climate, kids can garden all year long! In addition, planting in both the garden and in the greenhouse offers kids valuable opportunities to compare and contrast growing conditions. That will make little farmers of them all!

6   Our children can reap many rewards from a greenhouse. I hope I've succeeded in planting that idea in your head. If so, please cast your vote for a new greenhouse at our next school budget meeting.

Sincerely,

Margareta Flores, Parent

A greenhouse like the ones shown here would be a welcome addition to Washington Elementary.

Ambrose Hill School in our neighboring town already has a greenhouse. The students love it!

Prepare to Read

GENRE STUDY **Informational texts** give facts and examples about a topic.

- Authors of informational texts may organize their ideas using headings and subheadings.

- Authors of informational texts may organize their ideas by central ideas. Each central idea is supported by key details.

- Informational texts include visuals, such as charts, diagrams, graphs, timelines, and maps.

- Social studies texts include words that are specific to the topic.

SET A PURPOSE **Think about** the title and the genre of this text. What do you think you are going to learn from this text? Write your ideas below.

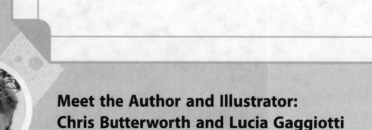

Meet the Author and Illustrator:
Chris Butterworth and Lucia Gaggiotti

CRITICAL VOCABULARY

stalk

dairy

curds

tingly

scarlet

grove

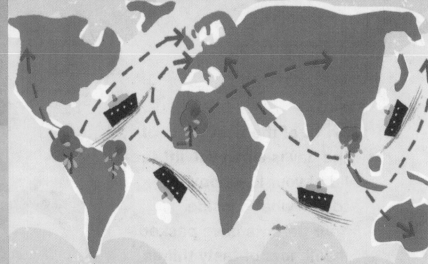

HOW DID THAT GET IN MY LUNCHBOX?

THE STORY OF FOOD

by Chris Butterworth

illustrated by Lucia Gaggiotti

1 **ONE** of the best parts of
the day is when you lift the
lid of your lunchbox
to see what's inside.
Your parents have packed
it with lots of tasty things
to eat. They probably
got all the food from
a grocery store—but food
doesn't grow in stores!

2 So where did it come from *before* it was in the store?

3 Just how **DID** all this food get in your lunchbox?

HOW DID THE **BREAD** IN YOUR SANDWICH GET IN YOUR LUNCHBOX?

4 A farmer planted seeds in spring,
and by summer they'd grown into tall,
waving wheat with fat, ripe grains at
the tip of every **stalk**.

5 The farmer cut the wheat with a
giant combine harvester and sent
it to a flour mill.

stalk   A stalk is the main stem of a plant.

288

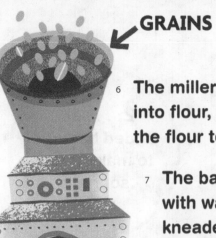

GRAINS

6 The miller ground the grains into flour, and trucks took the flour to a bakery.

YEAST

SUGAR

7 The baker mixed the flour with water, sugar, and yeast; kneaded it into a soft, squishy dough; and baked it in a very hot oven.

WATER

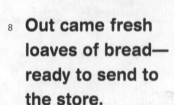

FLOUR

8 Out came fresh loaves of bread—ready to send to the store.

9 Take a bite of the bread in your sandwich—**MMMMMM,** crusty on the outside and soft in the middle!

HOW DID THE CHEESE IN YOUR SANDWICH GET IN YOUR LUNCHBOX?

10 Your cheese was once milk that came from a cow. A farmer milked the cows, and a tanker from the **dairy** came to collect the milk.

> **dairy** A dairy is a place where milk is prepared for drinking or is made into other products, like butter, cream, and cheese.

2. . . . and added bacteria to make it turn sour and thick.

11 1. In the dairy, cheese makers warmed up the milk . . .

5. They drained off the whey, chopped up the rubbery curds, added some salt, and pressed them into blocks.

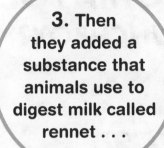

3. Then they added a substance that animals use to digest milk called rennet . . .

4. . . . and it changed again into bits called **curds**, floating in whey.

6. They stored the blocks for months until the cheese was ripe.

12 **Bite into your cheese—it's creamy and smooth, but tasty, too—and TINGLY on your tongue!**

curds Curds are the lumps that form in milk when it turns sour.
tingly Something that feels tingly stings a little or feels prickly.

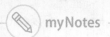

HOW DID YOUR **TOMATOES**
GET IN YOUR LUNCHBOX?

13 Last summer, your tomatoes were growing in a big plastic tunnel full of tomato plants.

14 The sun and the warmth made the plants grow tall and bloom with yellow flowers. As each flower died, a tiny green tomato fruit began to grow from its middle.

15 **Day by day, the plants sucked up water and the tomatoes swelled from green to orange to red.**

16 **When bunches of ripe, scarlet tomatoes dangled from the branches, the grower picked them, sorted them, packed them, and sent them to the store.**

17 **POP one in your mouth and squish the sweet-sour juice out!**

scarlet If something is scarlet, it is a bright red color.

293

HOW DID YOUR APPLE JUICE GET IN YOUR LUNCHBOX?

18   Last spring, the apple trees in the orchard were full of flowers. In summer, tiny apple buds grew from each flower stalk. The buds kept growing, and by autumn the trees were full of ripe, sweet fruit.

19   Pickers climbed into the trees and filled their bins with fruit.

294

20 **A truck took the bins to the juice factory where sorters threw out any rotten apples.**

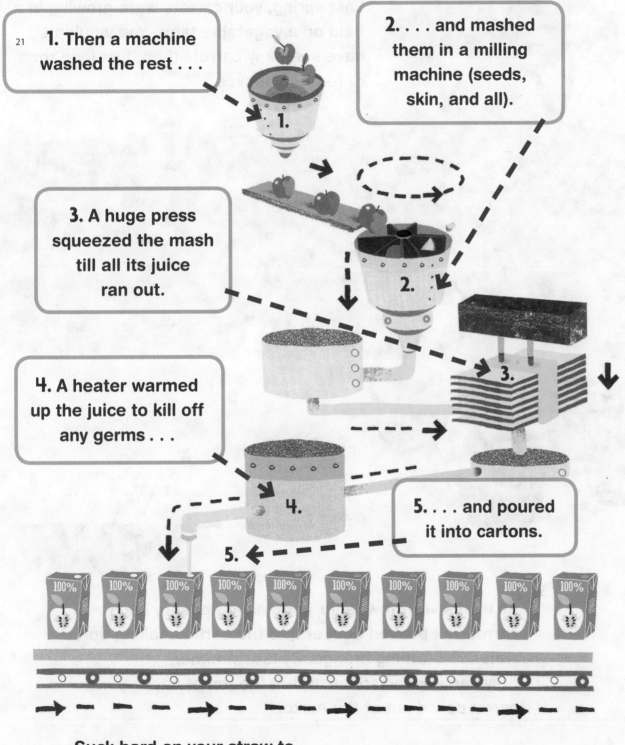

21 **1. Then a machine washed the rest . . .**

2. . . . and mashed them in a milling machine (seeds, skin, and all).

3. A huge press squeezed the mash till all its juice ran out.

4. A heater warmed up the juice to kill off any germs . . .

5. . . . and poured it into cartons.

1.

2.

3.

4.

5.

100% 100% 100% 100% 100% 100% 100% 100% 100% 100%

22 **Suck hard on your straw to taste the apple TANG!**

HOW DID YOUR CARROTS
GET IN YOUR LUNCHBOX?

23 Last spring, your carrots were growing in a field on a vegetable farm. You wouldn't have seen any carrots then, just long rows of feathery leaves.

24 As the leaves grew taller in the summer sun, each carrot root pushed deeper into the earth, soaking up water and turning orange. By late summer, they had swelled so much that the top of each carrot poked out of the earth.

25 Pickers pulled them up.

26 **Then the carrots were washed . . .**

and packed into trucks.

27 **Bite into your carrot— see just how SWEET and CRUNCHY it tastes!**

HOW DID YOUR **CLEMENTINE** GET IN YOUR LUNCHBOX?

28 **Early in summer, the trees in the clementine grove were full of sweet-smelling, waxy flowers.**

29 **As the flowers died, a tiny green clementine berry began to grow out of each one.**

30 **The clementines swelled in the warm sun, turning from green to yellow. By the time cooler winter weather arrived, the clementines had turned orange and were so heavy and full of juice that they made the branches droop.**

> **grove**   A grove is a group of trees that are close to one another.

31 **Pickers climbed ladders to reach them. They had to wear gloves so they didn't bruise the tender fruit inside the skin.**

32 **They washed them and packed them, and the grower sent the boxes in trucks to the market.**

33 **It's easy to peel a clementine! Then all you have to do is pop the JUICY pieces into your mouth and bite: most clementines are seedless!**

299

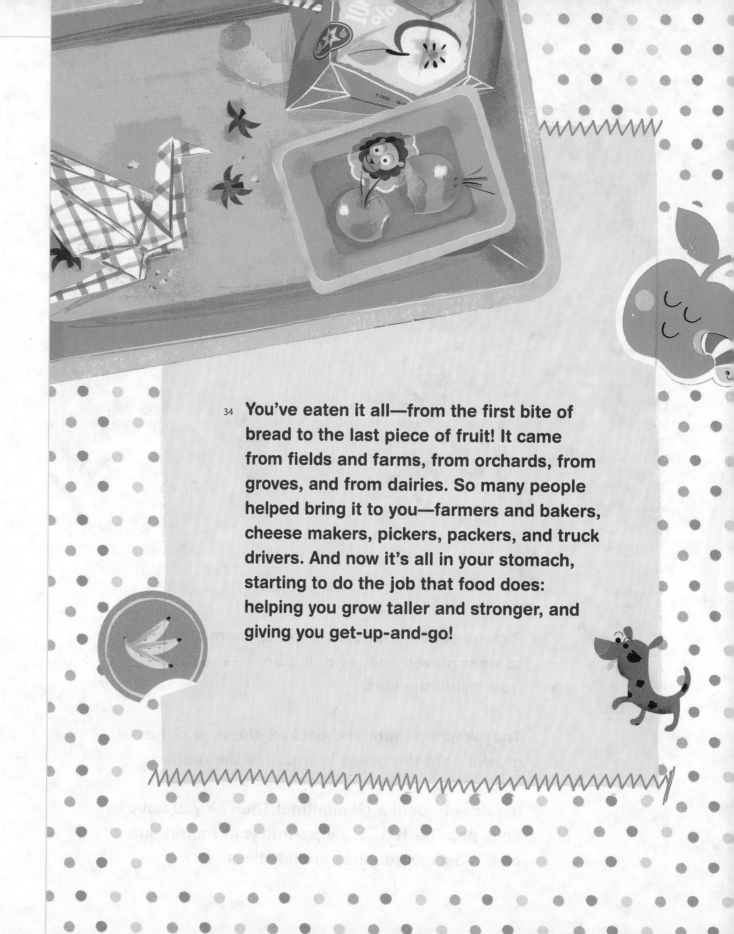

34 **You've eaten it all—from the first bite of bread to the last piece of fruit! It came from fields and farms, from orchards, from groves, and from dairies. So many people helped bring it to you—farmers and bakers, cheese makers, pickers, packers, and truck drivers. And now it's all in your stomach, starting to do the job that food does: helping you grow taller and stronger, and giving you get-up-and-go!**

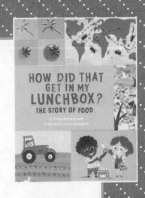

Collaborative Discussion

Look back at what you wrote on page 284. With a partner discuss what you learned from the text. Then work with a group to discuss the questions below. Refer to details in *How Did That Get in My Lunchbox?* to support your ideas. Take notes for your responses. Use your notes to connect the ideas you share to the comments made by others in your group.

1. Reread pages 288–289. Which workers help to make wheat into bread?

2. Review pages 296–297. How do farmers know when it is time to pick carrots?

3. What are some of the different jobs people do to make the food we all eat?

Write a Critique

PROMPT ....

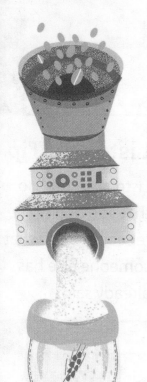

How Did That Get in My Lunchbox? uses words and pictures to tell how different foods make their way from farms, orchards, and dairies to markets or grocery stores. These foods are parts of the meals we eat.

Imagine you were given a free copy of this book in exchange for providing a critique, or feedback, to the publisher. The publisher is most interested in hearing how you feel about the way illustrations are used in this text to share information. Write a paragraph that tells your opinion about the illustration that shows the steps of making cheese. What did you learn about how cheese is made? Is this a good way to share important information? Why or why not?

PLAN ....

Make a list of things you like about the illustration. Then make a list of things you do not like about it. Compare the lists to help you decide what to tell the publisher.

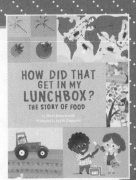

WRITE

Now write your critique of the cheese illustration.

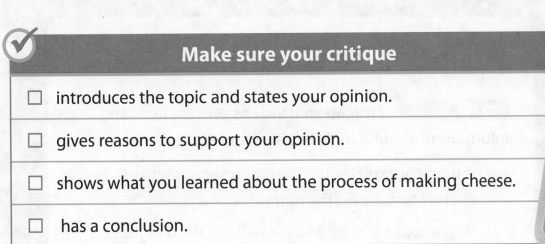

Make sure your critique
☐ introduces the topic and states your opinion.
☐ gives reasons to support your opinion.
☐ shows what you learned about the process of making cheese.
☐   has a conclusion.

Prepare to View

GENRE STUDY **Educational videos** present facts and information about a topic in visual and audio form.

- A narrator explains the topic as images on the screen change to support the narration.

- Real people, places, and animals are used in the videos to help viewers understand the topic.

- Like informational texts, educational videos include words that may be specific to a science or social studies topic.

- Producers of videos may include sound effects or music in the background.

SET A PURPOSE **Think about** the genre and title of this video. What do you think you will learn from this video? Write your ideas below.

Build Background: Organic Farming

CRITICAL VOCABULARY

rotation

prepping

storage

Carrots, Farm to Fork

As you watch *Carrots, Farm to Fork,* notice the real people and places shown in this video. Why do you think the video includes an interview with a real farmer? Pay careful attention to what he says and does to help you understand how carrots are grown and sold. Would it be as clear if you read an article on the same topic? Why or why not? Take notes in the space below.

As you watch, listen for the Critical Vocabulary words *rotation, prepping,* and *storage.* Listen for clues to the meaning of each word. Take notes in the space below about how each word is used.

rotation   If things are in rotation, they take turns doing a job or serving a purpose.
prepping   If you are prepping something, you are preparing it, or getting it ready, for the next step.
storage   When something is in storage, it is put away so it can be used later.

Respond to the Text

Collaborative Discussion

Look back at what you wrote on page 304. With a partner discuss what you learned from the video. Then work with a group to discuss the questions below. Refer to details in *Carrots, Farm to Fork* to support your ideas. Take notes for your responses.

1 What do carrots need to grow well?

2 How do carrots get from a farm to a family's table?

3 Why do people like buying vegetables that grow nearby?

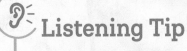

Listening Tip

Are you wondering about something that someone else said? Summarize what you think they meant, and ask if you're right.

Speaking Tip

Be sure to say each word clearly. It may help your listeners if you use vocabulary words that were explained in the video.

Write a Question and Answer Summary

In the video *Carrots, Farm to Fork*, farmer Matthew Martin describes how he began farming, the different kinds of work he does, and what he loves about his job.

You have been asked to write about the video for your class blog. Summarize the video by writing a list of questions that can be answered by the video, such as "What kind of soil do carrots need to grow?" or "What does Matthew Martin love about being a farmer?" Then provide an answer for each based on facts and details found in the video.

Make a list of the most important facts and details you saw in the video. List some facts and details about both Matthew Martin and about carrots.

Carrots, Farm to Fork

Now write your blog post that summarizes the video in a question-and-answer format.

✓ Make sure your blog post
☐ has an introduction.
☐ is organized in a question-and-answer format.
☐ includes facts and details from the video.
☐ includes a conclusion.

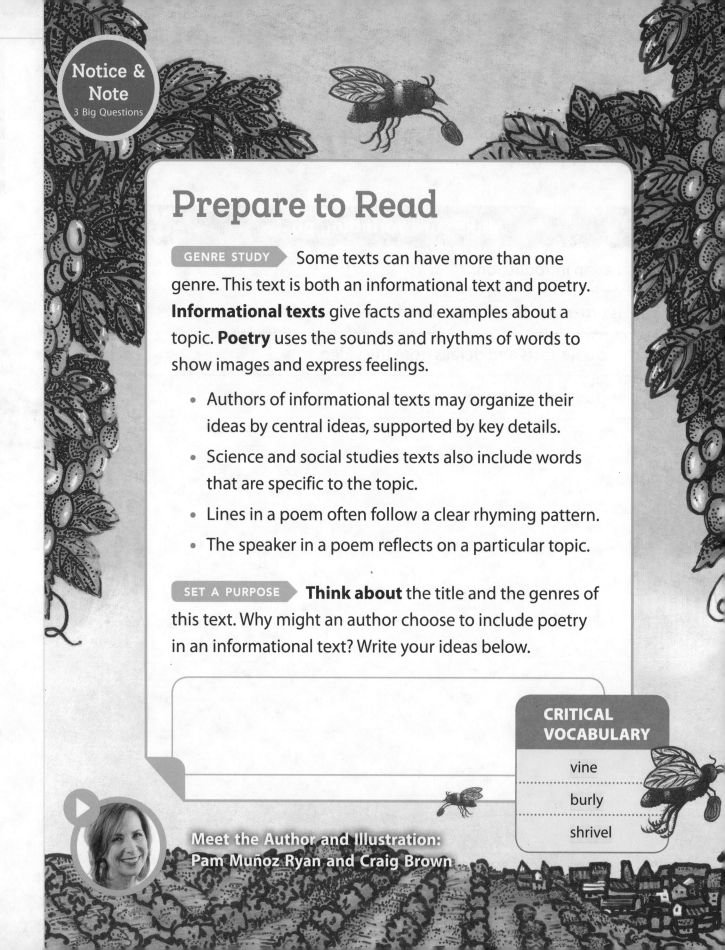

Prepare to Read

GENRE STUDY Some texts can have more than one genre. This text is both an informational text and poetry. **Informational texts** give facts and examples about a topic. **Poetry** uses the sounds and rhythms of words to show images and express feelings.

- Authors of informational texts may organize their ideas by central ideas, supported by key details.
- Science and social studies texts also include words that are specific to the topic.
- Lines in a poem often follow a clear rhyming pattern.
- The speaker in a poem reflects on a particular topic.

SET A PURPOSE **Think about** the title and the genres of this text. Why might an author choose to include poetry in an informational text? Write your ideas below.

CRITICAL VOCABULARY

vine

burly

shrivel

Meet the Author and Illustration:
Pam Muñoz Ryan and Craig Brown

How Do You Raise a Raisin?

by **Pam Muñoz Ryan**

illustrated by **Craig Brown**

1 How do you raise a raisin?
Tell me so I'll know.
They're such peculiar little things.
How do they sprout and grow?
Do raisins grow on Earth, or other planets, far away?
Do aliens collect them and space-shuttle them our way?

2 Raisins are dried grapes. So far, there is no proof that raisins grow on other planets. Raisins ARE grown on Earth, in countries like Turkey, Iran, Greece, Australia, and the United States.

3 So, who discovered raisins?
Were they here when Earth began?
Who **WAS** the first to nibble them—dinosaur or man?

4 Raisins were probably discovered when someone or someTHING tasted grapes that had dried on the vine. Over the years people and animals figured out which grapes produced the sweetest, yummiest raisins.

> **vine**   A vine is a long, thin stem of a plant that grows along the ground or up and around something.

myNotes

312

5 Do raisins grow in **one** place, like Raisin Creek or Raisin Hill? Is there a special town called Raisinfield or Raisinville?

6 Raisins grow best in areas with nice dirt, many days of hot weather, a dry climate, and plenty of water. Almost all of the raisins in the United States are grown in the San Joaquin Valley of California, near towns like Chowchilla, Dinuba, Kingsburg, Selma, Weedpatch, and even Raisin City! About 90 percent of the raisins sold in the United States come from the area around Fresno, California.

7 Do farmers plant some seeds from the local garden shop? And wait for raisin bushes to produce a raisin crop?

8 Farmers start a new crop of raisins by taking "cuttings" from an older grapevine. These pieces of stem are planted in sand until they sprout. Then, they are planted in the fields, next to a wooden stake.

Raisinville, USA

9 **Notice how the grapevines and the sprawling branches grow. Does a grapevine tamer train them into picture-perfect rows?**

10 Grapevines are grown about eight feet apart. Fieldworkers hand-tie the sturdy branches, or "canes," to rows of wire. There are usually two sets of wire, a top set that is about six feet high, and a second wire that is three or four feet high.

11 **How long do raisins take to grow? A week, a month, or a year? How many hours must you wait for a raisin to appear?**

12 It takes at least three years until the vines are old enough for the first crop of raisins. That's 26,280 hours!

13 **When grapes are ripe and ready, how do farmers get them down? Do they rent a burly giant to shake them to the ground?**

14 When the grapes are ready, skilled grape-pickers snag the grape clusters from the vines using a sharp vine-cutter.

15 Most grapes are turned into raisins the same way they've been for thousands of years: they are left to dry naturally in the sun.

burly Someone who is burly is big and strong.

16 What do raisins lie on
while they're basking in the sun?
Do they rest on little beach towels
until they're dried and done?

17 The grape clusters are laid on brown paper
trays on the ground between the grapevine
rows. This is called "laying the grapes
down." The sun rises in the east and sets
in the west. Most raisin growers plant
their vineyards in east-to-west rows. This
way, grapes drying between the rows
receive the most sun. If they were drying
in north-to-south rows, the grapes would
be in the shade part of the day, and when
it comes to raising raisins, the more sun
the better.

18 How long do clusters lie around
to sweeten, dry, and bake?
How many weeks in the valley
heat does raisin-making take?

19 Raisins bake in the sun for about two
to three weeks. Then, the paper trays
are rolled into bundles that look like
burritos and are left in the field for a
few more days to make sure that all the
raisins are dry.

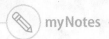
20 Raisins do not look like grapes—they're withered up and wrinkled! Are they soaked inside a bathtub until their skin is crinkled?

21 As grapes bake in the hot sun, their water evaporates. The more water they lose, the more the grapes shrivel, causing wrinkles.

> **shrivel** When things shrivel, they dry out and get smaller and wrinkled.

22 How many grapes must a farmer dry upon the valley ground? To make a box of raisins that weighs about one pound?

23 It takes about four and one-half pounds of fresh grapes to make one pound of raisins.

24 Who puts raisins in the boxes that keep them sweet and dried? Do tiny fairy princesses stuff each one inside?

25 When they're needed, raisin bins are brought into the factory for packaging. It takes only ten minutes from bin to package! Workers and machines take off the stems and capstems, sort, and wash the raisins. Then the raisins are packaged in a variety of boxes and bags.

26 **What happens to the raisins that aren't the very best? Are they sent to raisin prep school until they pass the test?**

27 When it comes to raisins, nothing is wasted! The stems and capstems are ground up and used for animal feed. Raisins that are not perfect are made into raisin concentrate that's used as a natural preservative in cakes, breads, and cookies. The best raisins are used for eating, baking, and adding to cereals.

1. Get plenty of sun.
2. Roll over after two weeks.
3. Dry evenly.

28 **Raisins taste so very sweet, but they're considered "sugar-free." Is each one dipped in a honey pot by a busy honeybee?**

29 Raisins are naturally sweet!

30 For centuries, people have valued raisins. Scientists who planned the space shuttle menus knew that raisins are the perfect fast food for long journeys. They are lightweight, don't spoil easily, satisfy the craving for something sweet, and provide nutrition and energy.

Collaborative Discussion

How Do You Raise a Raisin?
by Pam Muñoz Ryan
Illustrated by Craig Brown

Look back at what you wrote on page 310. With a partner discuss your ideas about why the author chose to include poetry. Then work with a group to discuss the questions below. Refer to details in *How Do You Raise a Raisin?* to support your ideas. Take notes for your responses. During your discussion, take turns and make sure everyone's ideas are heard.

1. Review pages 314–315. What parts of growing raisins take hard work? What parts take a lot of waiting?

2. Reread pages 317–318. What are some of the ways people use raisins?

3. How do the poems connect to the informational text? What is the author's reason for including the poems?

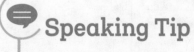

Listening Tip

Look at each speaker and listen closely. Do you understand the idea each speaker shares?

Speaking Tip

If you would like more information, ask a question, such as, *Can you tell me more about…?*

Write an Opinion Essay

PROMPT

In *How Do You Raise a Raisin?*, the author uses vivid imagery and a question and answer format to tell readers facts about raisins in an engaging way. She asks questions using rhyming poetry and then answers them in ordinary prose.

Write an essay that gives examples of the most vivid imagery in *How Do You Raise a Raisin?* Then tell which examples you like best. Give reasons to support your opinion. Try to use some of the Critical Vocabulary words in your writing.

PLAN

Make a list of phrases in the text that create a vivid image in your mind. When your list is complete, circle your favorites.

WRITE

Now write your opinion essay about the text's vivid imagery.

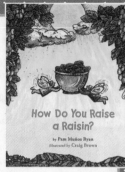

Make sure your opinion essay

☐ begins with an introduction and ends with a conclusion.

☐ includes examples of imagery from the text.

☐ states your opinion.

☐ gives reasons for your opinion.

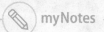

Notice & Note
3 Big Questions

Prepare to Read

GENRE STUDY **Informational texts** give facts and examples about a topic.

- Authors of informational texts may present their ideas in sequential, or chronological, order. This helps readers understand what happens and when.

- Science texts include words that are specific to the topic. These are words that name things or ideas.

SET A PURPOSE **Think about** the title and genre of this text, and look at the photographs. What do you think you will learn from this text? Write your ideas below.

Meet the Author and Photographer: George Ancona

CRITICAL VOCABULARY

layout

arbor

transplanted

mulch

blooming

kernels

IT'S OUR GARDEN

From Seeds to Harvest in a School Garden

❀ by George Ancona ❀

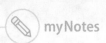

The school bell sounds . . .

1 and the classrooms explode with the noise of books closing, chairs sliding on the floor, and kids chattering. It's time for recess! The students head outside to the school garden.

2 Mrs. McCarthy, the third-grade teacher, dreamed of having a school garden. She talked to the other teachers, the principal, and the parents about it. They all worked together to make her dream come true. The garden is cared for by Miss Sue.

3 Miss Sue's husband, Will, designed the layout of the garden. College students Paul, Danielle, Autumn, and Allie volunteer to guide the children in the garden projects.

> **layout** A layout is a drawing or plan that shows where things are or will be.

4   Students enter the garden through an arbor. It's spring, and there are lots of chores to be done. Depending on the weather, some classes are held in the open classroom, the garden, or the greenhouse.

5   In early spring, Miss Sue asks the students to make a book with pictures they cut out from seed catalogs. These are the flowers, fruits, and vegetables that the students would like to grow. Later, she and the students will decide where to plant them.

> **arbor**   An arbor is a shady passageway made of vines or branches.

6   Every day, one student is asked to take a bucket of food scraps from lunches and snacks and dump it into the compost pile.

7   The compost is made up of soil, dead plants, and food scraps. Inside the pile, red wriggler worms are busy eating and turning these ingredients into castings. Compost is mixed into the garden beds to provide food for seedlings.

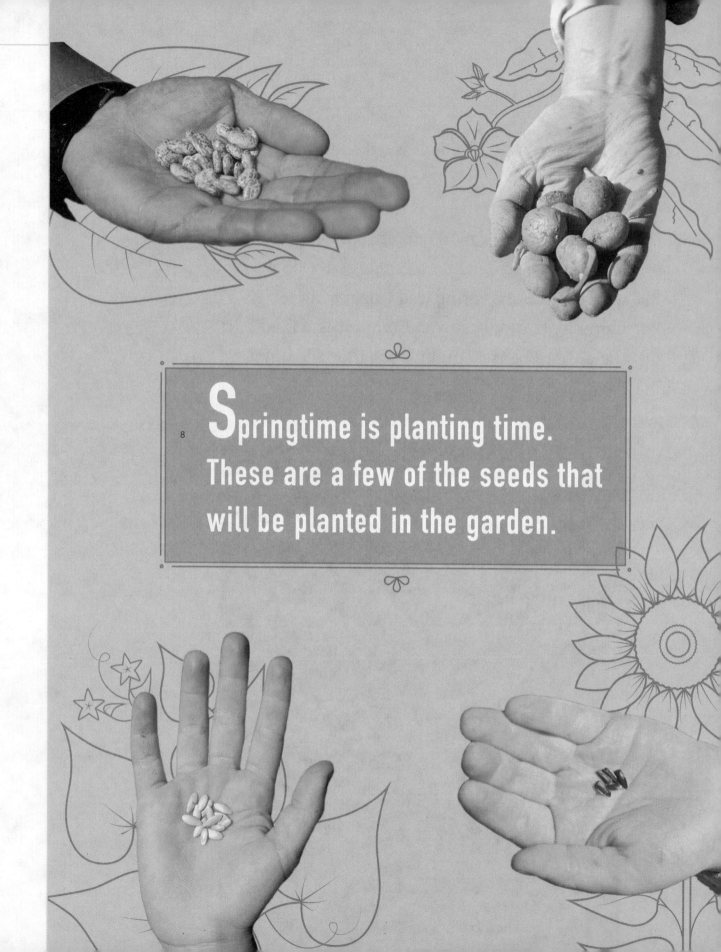

8 **S**pringtime is planting time. These are a few of the seeds that will be planted in the garden.

9   When it's still cold outside, some seeds are planted in the greenhouse. There, students fill small plastic pots with rich soil and plant a seed in each. The pots are left in the greenhouse. The sun warms them. Soon, tiny seedlings begin to pop out of the soil. When they are bigger and the weather is warmer, the plants will be transplanted into the garden beds outside.

10   Flowers, vegetables, and fruits are planted in the beds of rich composted earth. A tepee made of bamboo poles stands in the middle of the garden. Some students plant pole-bean seeds at the base of each pole. The plants will grow up the tepee and sprout their pods.

---

transplanted   If you transplanted something, you took it from the place it was growing and planted it in a new place.

11   Meanwhile, in the morning shade of the
school, Paul hands out seeds to plant in a waffle
bed. The bed's low walls of adobe bricks help
keep water in.

12   Another group of students plants squash
seedlings. Danielle helps a student transplant a
tomato seedling. Once the seeds and seedlings
are in the ground, the beds are watered and
covered with a mulch of straw. This helps to
keep the soil from drying out.

13   A lot of water is needed to keep the garden
healthy. When it rains, water flows off the roof,
down a drainpipe, and into an underground
tank called a cistern. A solar panel on the roof

mulch   If you put mulch in your garden, you put straw or
wood chips around your plants to help protect them.

of the outdoor classroom creates electricity to run the pump that draws water from the cistern. One of the students' favorite jobs is watering the garden. Miss Sue fills the colorful watering cans for them.

14   The tomato plants are surrounded by plastic tubes filled with water. During the day, the sun warms the water in the tubes. At night, the tubes provide the warmth that tomato roots need to grow. When there is no rainwater in the cistern, a hose attached to an outdoor faucet is used to keep the soil moist and plants healthy.

15   While the plants are growing during the warm spring days, there is still a lot of work to do in the garden. Students mix sand, dirt, water, and cut-up straw to make adobe bricks. The bricks are used to make the low walls for waffle beds. In the Southwest, adobe bricks are still used to build homes.

16   Adobe is also used to coat the *horno*, the traditional oven used to bake bread. Every spring, the *horno* in the corner of the outdoor classroom gets a fresh coat of adobe.

17   There are many different plants in the herb garden, such as basil, chives, and sage. Every plant has its own taste and smell.

18   Radishes are harvested in the spring. Miss Sue asks some students to pick the radishes. After washing the dirt off them, the children bite into the bright-red vegetables. One girl finds hers too spicy and drops it into the compost pile. More food for the worms!

19   On special afternoons and weekends, the garden becomes a place where the school community gathers. Students come back with their family and friends. They compost, seed, plant, transplant, weed, water, and dig. By now, the flowers are blooming and the beds are green. The garden is flourishing with so much care.

20   Garden chores continue into summer. School is closed, but the garden is a beehive of activity. It provides the setting for music and gatherings of children, grownups, friends, and families. The music fills the garden with joy.

blooming   When trees or plants are blooming, their flowers are out and open.

21   By August, many of the fruits and vegetables
are ripe. Cooking and eating becomes an
ongoing activity in the garden.

22   A father helps the children make pizzas on
one community day. First they mix and punch
the dough. Then they roll it out with a rolling
pin. Next they pour oil on the flat dough. Ripe
tomatoes are cut up and go on top. And last, of
course, is the grated cheese.

23   After a hot fire burns down in the *horno*, the
pizza goes in. When the sizzling pizza is taken
out, a group of hungry gardeners appears. The
slices disappear like magic. Fortunately, there
are many more pizzas to come.

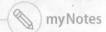

24   Summer is over, and another school year begins. The leaves on the trees are turning color, and many of the garden's fruits and vegetables are ready to be picked. Students take turns disappearing into the tepee to pick pole beans from the vines.

25   One of the garden beds was planted in a traditional Native American way. It's called a three-sisters garden. Corn is planted together with pinto beans and squash. The bean vines grow up the cornstalks. The corn and squash leaves shade the soil to keep it moist. Pinto beans are harvested after the pods dry up and turn tan.

26   Cabbages are a real challenge to pick. Their long, strong roots test the strength of some of the bigger kids.

27   Lemon cucumbers, also called apple cucumbers, are a new experience for most of the students. The children like them because they can be eaten like apples.

28 In the three-sisters garden, the strawberry corn is ready for harvesting. The ears are taken off of the stalks and husked. Then the kernels are picked off the cob and saved in a jar.

29 Later, the kernels are heated in oil and turned into a delicious popcorn snack. The students are delighted.

30 The harvest becomes a chance for Miss Sue to quiz the students on the variety of crops the garden has produced. She makes a game of the quiz, placing the answers face down on slips of paper under each fruit, vegetable, or herb.

> **kernels**   Kernels are the grains or seeds of plants such as corn or wheat.

31   To celebrate the end of the harvest, a series of lunches is prepared with many of the garden's vegetables. These become festivals of good food and fun.

32   The last community day of the year brings students and families together to prepare the garden for winter. The air is crisp and cold. Frost has turned the trees to gold. Winds have scattered many leaves to the ground. The green plants of summer are shriveled and brown. Dead plants are yanked out of the ground and put into the compost pile.

33   Compost is strained and mixed into the soil. The strawberry plants and beds are mulched with straw. And all is ready to be covered with a blanket of snow. Sleep tight, garden!

34   **Until next year!**

Collaborative Discussion

Look back at what you wrote on page 322. With a partner discuss what you learned from the text. Then work with a group to discuss the questions below. Refer to details in *It's Our Garden* to support your ideas. Take notes for your responses. Be sure you understand what others in your group are saying and that they understand you, too.

1 Reread page 326. Why do the students look through seed catalogs? How will this help them?

2 Review pages 330–331. How do the students get the water they use to water their plants?

3 What are some of the ways that fruits and vegetables from the garden are used?

Listening Tip

If you don't understand what someone else has said, ask a question! You can also ask the speaker to talk more slowly or a little louder.

Speaking Tip

Help group members understand what you are saying by speaking at a pace that isn't too fast or too slow.

Write an Instruction Manual

In *It's Our Garden*, the author describes what the children, parents, and other volunteers do to make their school garden a success. There is much work to be done in every season of the year!

Imagine that you have been asked to write an instruction manual for new volunteers at the school garden. Write a paragraph that explains the tasks and activities that happen in the garden during each season of the year. Don't forget to use some of the Critical Vocabulary words in your writing.

Divide this space into four boxes. In each box, list the tasks that must be completed during a different season of the year.

WRITE ....

Now write your instruction manual that describes the tasks that must be done in the garden during each season.

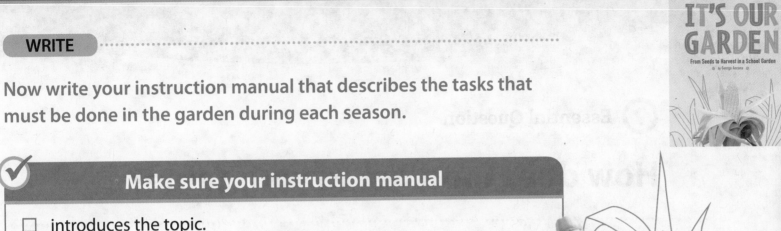

IT'S OUR GARDEN
From Seeds to Harvest in a School Garden
by George Ancona

✓ **Make sure your instruction manual**

☐ introduces the topic.

☐ summarizes the garden tasks that happen in all four seasons.

☐ is organized in a logical way.

☐ uses transition words like *then*, *next*, and *after* between topics.

☐ uses linking words like *also, another, and,* or *more* to connect related ideas.

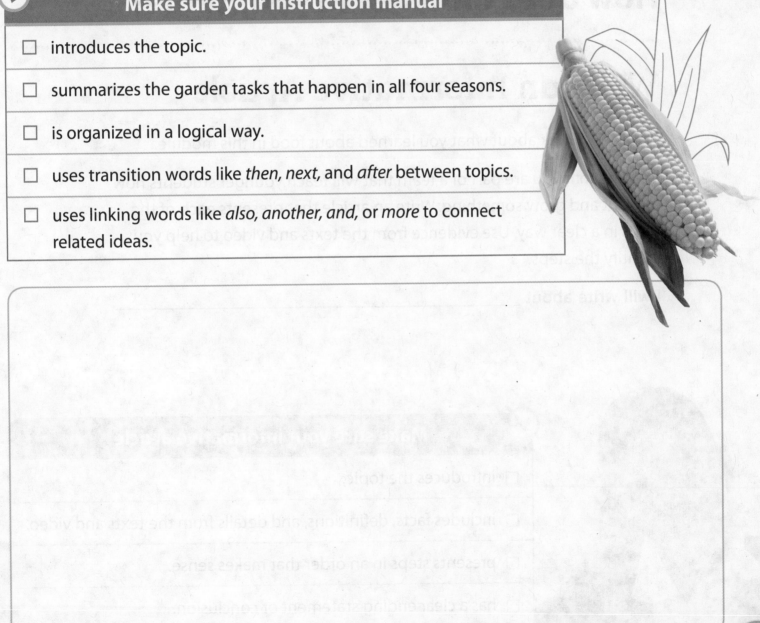

Performance Task

? Essential Question

How does food get to your table?

Write an Informative Article

PROMPT Think about what you learned about food in this module.

Imagine that you are part of a team that will teach younger students how to plant and grow something. Write an article that presents each of the steps in a clear way. Use evidence from the texts and video to help you identify the steps.

I will write about _____.

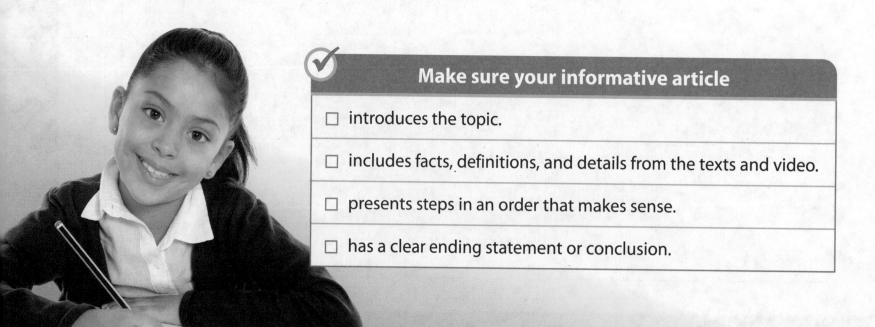

Make sure your informative article

☐ introduces the topic.

☐ includes facts, definitions, and details from the texts and video.

☐ presents steps in an order that makes sense.

☐ has a clear ending statement or conclusion.

PLAN .... **Gather information.**

What will you explain how to grow? What steps do you need to include? Look back at your notes and review the texts and video for ideas.

Plan your article in the chart below. Write a central idea sentence that states your topic and tells what you will explain. Then use evidence from the texts and video to list the steps you will include. Use Critical Vocabulary words where you can.

My Topic: ______________________________

Central Idea

↓

Steps
1.
2.
3.
4.

DRAFT ·· Write your informative article.

Use the information you wrote in the graphic organizer on page 345 to draft your informative article.

Introduce your topic in a clear way. Get readers interested so they will want to find out more.

List the steps for planting and growing something in the **body** of your article. Use linking words, such as *first, next,* and *last,* to connect the steps.

End by reviewing what you have explained. Give readers some ideas for how to use their first crop!

The revision and editing steps give you a chance to look carefully at your writing and make changes. Work with a partner to determine whether you have explained your ideas clearly to readers. Use these questions to help you evaluate and improve your report.

✓ PURPOSE/ FOCUS	ORGANIZATION	EVIDENCE	LANGUAGE/ VOCABULARY	CONVENTIONS
☐ Does my article state the topic in a clear way? ☐ Did I include each important step?	☐ Do I list the steps in an order that makes sense? ☐ Did I begin and end in an interesting way?	☐ Did I support my central idea with evidence from the texts and video?	☐ Did I use clear, exact words to explain each step?	☐ Are all the words spelled correctly? ☐ Did I use commas and end punctuation correctly?

PUBLISH ·· Share your work.

Create a Finished Copy Make a final copy of your article. You may want to include a photo or drawing of the plant you chose. Consider these options to share your article:

1. Combine your article with those of your classmates to create a "Guide to Growing" display for younger students.

2. Read your article to your classmates. Invite them to comment and ask questions.

3. Make a video to show the steps you describe in your article. Post the video on a school or class website.

Tell a Tale

"Language grows out
of life, out of its needs
and experiences."

—Anne Sullivan

Get Curious
Video

Words About Telling Tales

The words in the chart below will help you talk and write about the selections in this module. Which words about telling tales have you seen before? Which words are new to you?

Add to the Vocabulary Network on page 351 by writing synonyms, antonyms, and related words and phrases for each word.

After you read each selection in this module, come back to the Vocabulary Network and keep building it. Add more ovals if you need to.

WORD	MEANING	CONTEXT SENTENCE
myth (noun)	A myth is a well-known story about fantastical events that happened in the past.	We read a myth about the unicorns that once lived in the woods.
folklore (noun)	Folklore is the traditional sayings, beliefs, and stories within a community.	They performed a dance that was part of our folklore.
recount (verb)	If you recount a story or events, you tell how something happened.	One day, my mom will recount the stories she learned from her mom.
inherit (verb)	When you inherit something, it is given to you, usually by a parent or grandparent.	Someday, Sheena will inherit the jewelry her grandmother leaves her.

myth

folklore

recount

inherit

Words About Telling Tales

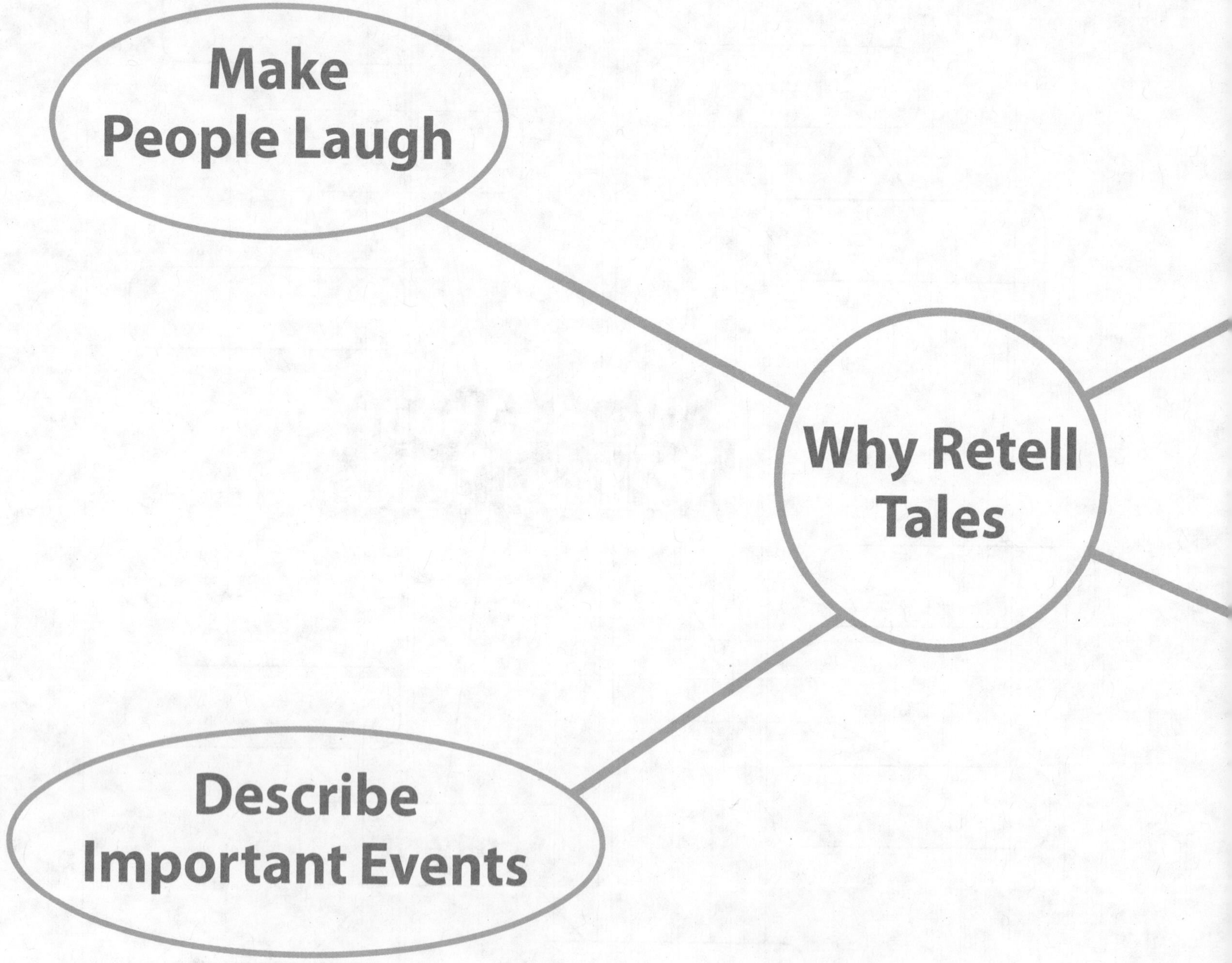

Make
People Laugh

Why Retell
Tales

Describe
Important Events

Teach an Important Lesson

Tell About a Culture's Beliefs

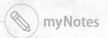
Short Read

Why We Share Stories

1   You probably know some stories that have been passed down over time. For example, there's the tale of Cinderella, who loses a glass slipper and finds a prince. You may also know about Jack, the boy who climbs a beanstalk and stands up to a mean giant. Both of these tales have been around for many, many years.

2   Why do people tell certain stories again and again? People might tell stories to teach lessons about the right way to behave. They might share stories about a people's history. A story might recount, or tell about, how something came to be. It might tell about a hero or give advice. All these stories together make up a people's folklore.

3   People often pass down stories that teach lessons. For example, Cinderella is good-hearted and hardworking, and she is rewarded with true love. Jack, the beanstalk climber, is brave and adventurous, and he is rewarded with treasure. In the African folktale "Jackal and Lion," a jackal is stalked by a hungry lion. The jackal uses his wits to escape. Not being eaten—that's his reward! The story teaches us we can solve problems with our wits. Lessons like these never get old.

4   Long ago, when people had a question about how the world works, they'd make up a myth, legend, or folktale to explain it. For example, the Native American tale "Crow Brings the Daylight" tells a story about the sun's movements. In the story, the Arctic, the land of the north, is always dark. Then Crow goes to the warm lands of the south and brings back light. Even though science now explains how the sun affects Earth, people still love to share this story. Long ago, it helped the people of the Arctic explain why the sun is in the sky.

5   Above all, stories have to be entertaining. Otherwise, people would not retell them. Boring stories become forgotten over time. Long ago, stories brought people together and helped distract them from the day's worries. The funnier or more exciting the story, the better. One example is the Native American tale "Coyote and Turtle Run a Race." It tells how Turtle tricked Coyote and beat him in a footrace. It has been making people laugh for generations.

6   If you're lucky, you may inherit some stories from your own people. Your people are probably your family, but they might also be the people in your town, in your school, or any group you spend time with. If you do hear a good story, be sure to pass it on. Every time you share a story, you are helping to keep it alive.

Prepare to Read

GENRE STUDY **Legends** are stories from the past that are believed by many people but cannot be proven to be true.

- Authors of legends tell the story through the plot.
- The events of a legend are thought to be based on real events.
- Authors of legends use sensory details and figurative language to develop the setting and the characters.
- Legends include the beliefs and ideas of a culture.

SET A PURPOSE **Think about** the title and genre of this text, and look at the illustrations. What events do you think this legend is about? Write your ideas below.

**Meet the Author and Illustrator:
Celia Godkin**

CRITICAL VOCABULARY

lagoon

garlands

belched

cinders

appease

barren

When the Giant Stirred

by Celia Godkin

1 Long, long ago
   in a blue, blue sea
   lay a green, green island.

2 On the island
   there were white, sandy beaches
   with coconut palms,
   where great sea turtles
   came by moonlight
   to bury their eggs in the sand.

3 On the island
   there were leafy, green forests
   with brightly colored butterflies,
   where noisy, red parrots
   screeched and chattered
   from the treetops.

4 On the island
   there was a cool, blue lagoon,
   where many silvery fish
   swam in an underwater garden
   of strange and wondrous animals.

> **lagoon** A lagoon is an area of seawater that
> is separated from the ocean by rocks or sand.

5   On the island
    there was a sleepy village
    of grass-thatched houses
    where gentle, smiling people
    went about their daily lives.

6   They collected
    coconuts from the beaches,
    fruit from the forest,
    and fish from the lagoon.

7   Over all of this peaceful island
    towered a great,
    cone-shaped mountain.
    Most of the time it was quiet,
    but sometimes
    it let out a puff of smoke
    or rumbled like a giant
    mumbling in his sleep.

8 When the giant stirred,
the people of the village
took garlands of flowers
up the mountain and threw them
in the crater at the top.
They prayed that the sweet,
heavy scent of the flowers
would put their mountain god
back to sleep
and give him pleasant dreams.

9 But there came a day
when the mountain
would not go back to sleep.
It rumbled and roared.
It belched out black smoke,
which fell as a rain of cinders
on the village.

garlands Garlands are ropes made of flowers or leaves.

belched If a volcano or chimney belched, it suddenly pushed out a large amount of smoke or fire.

cinders Cinders are small black pieces of ash that are left after a fire has burned.

10 The people were afraid
to go up the mountain.
Instead, they huddled fearfully
in their homes.

11 The parrots and all the other birds
flew screeching and chattering
up into the sky.
They made
a great, colorful, noisy cloud,
which flew away across the sea
in search of another island
on which to live.

12   The chief of the village
      gathered his people around him.
      He told them that the birds
      were the messengers of the gods.
      He said that, when the birds left,
      the mountain would awake in anger,
      and no amount of flowers
      would appease
      their mountain god now.

13   The chief told his people
      it was time to leave
      their beautiful island home.

14   The people did as they were told.
      They gathered their belongings
      and hurried with them to the beach.
      They loaded the boats
      and paddled away across the sea,
      looking for another island
      on which to live.

> **appease**   If you appease someone, you try to
> make the person less angry by giving in to what
> he or she wants.

15 For days after the people left,
the mountain
belched out black smoke.
It rumbled and roared
till the ground
shook and shook and shook.

16 Then—

17 The island people
heard the explosion
miles away across the sea.
They had just landed
on another island,
but they knew
they were not yet safe.
Their legends told them
the anger of the gods
stretched across oceans.

18 So they scrambled up
the mountainside
of their new island
as fast as they could go.
When they were safely out of reach,
they stopped and looked back
as a great tidal wave
swept toward them.

19 For days afterward
huge waves crashed against the shore.
For weeks afterward
the sky was black with smoke,
and cinders rained down from above.
But the people were safe
in their new island home,
and they began to build a village.

20 But what of the old island?

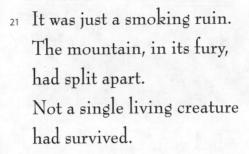

21 It was just a smoking ruin.
The mountain, in its fury,
had split apart.
Not a single living creature
had survived.

22 For many months, the island
was just a barren, black rock
in a blue, blue sea.

23 Little fishes swam around it,
and some found their way
into the lagoon.
Strange and wondrous animals
began to grow there.

24 One day,
some seeds blew over in the wind
and lodged in a crevice in the rock.
Little plants began to grow.
Later, bigger plants began to grow.

barren If an area of land is barren, it is dry and cannot grow plants or trees.

25   Storms washed white sand
up onto the shore.
Coconuts bobbed by in the water
and came to rest on the sand.
They put down roots
and began to grow
into coconut palms.

26   Then, great sea turtles
came by moonlight
to lay their eggs in the sand.
Weeks later, little hatching turtles
broke free from their nests
and scampered across the beach
into the sea.

27   Butterflies blew over on the wind
and found a home among the plants.
A pair of parrots flew by
and settled in the coconut palms.

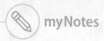

28 Month by month, year by year,
    plants and animals returned,
    until there were once again
    white, sandy beaches
    with coconut palms,
    leafy, green forests
    with brightly colored birds
    and butterflies,
    and a cool, blue lagoon,
    with silvery fish
    in an underwater garden
    of strange and wondrous animals.

29 Perhaps one day,
    there would be also
    a sleepy village
    of grass-thatched houses
    with gentle, smiling people.

30 For the legends say that,
    just as the mountain gods
    destroy themselves,
    so too are they reborn as islands,
    which rise out of the sea
    in an endless cycle of destruction
    and renewal.

Collaborative Discussion

Look back at what you wrote on page 356. With a partner discuss your ideas about the events the legend describes. Then work with a group to discuss the questions below. Refer to details in *When the Giant Stirred* to support your ideas. Take notes for your responses. Use your notes to connect your ideas to what others have said.

1 Review pages 360–361. What details in the text and illustration show you what life is like for the people on the island?

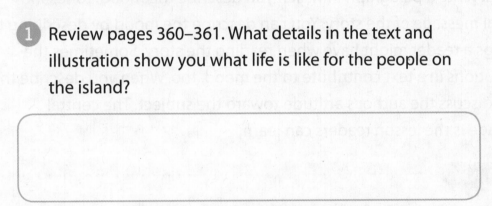

2 Reread pages 363–367. What are some reasons the people decide to leave their island?

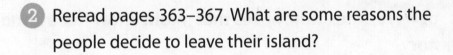

3 What forms of life return to the island after some time? What forms of life do not?

Listening Tip

Listen for the speaker's central idea in the discussion. Does the speaker include details that support that central idea?

Speaking Tip

State a central idea clearly. What details from the text and the illustrations can you name that support the central idea?

Write a Wiki Entry

PROMPT ....

When the Giant Stirred tells the story of an island that was destroyed by a volcano. Although the people and animals were driven away, after a while life returned to the island again.

Pretend you are writing an entry for *When the Giant Stirred* in a wiki about stories. Write a paragraph in which you describe the mood, tone, and central message of the story. You can describe the mood by describing the feelings a reader might have when reading the story. Sometimes the illustrations in a text contribute to the mood, too. When you describe the tone, discuss the author's attitude toward the subject. The central message is the lesson readers can learn.

PLAN ....

Make a list of feelings you had while reading the text. Make another list of words the author uses that might show her attitude toward the story.

Now write your wiki entry that describes the tone, mood, and central message of *When the Giant Stirred*.

Make sure your wiki entry

☐ describes the mood of the story.

☐ explains how the illustrations contribute to the mood of the story.

☐ identifies the tone of the story.

☐ tells the central message of the story.

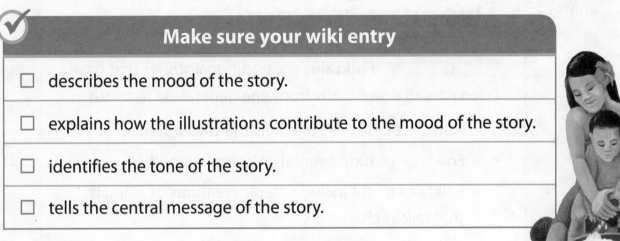

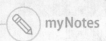

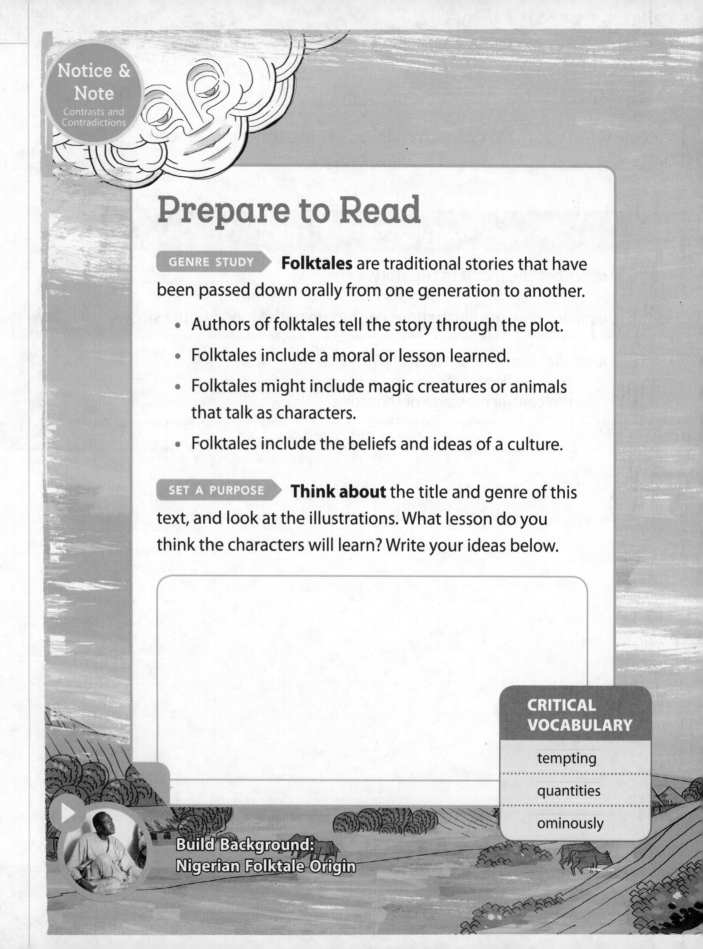

Notice &
Note
Contrasts and
Contradictions

Prepare to Read

GENRE STUDY **Folktales** are traditional stories that have been passed down orally from one generation to another.

- Authors of folktales tell the story through the plot.
- Folktales include a moral or lesson learned.
- Folktales might include magic creatures or animals that talk as characters.
- Folktales include the beliefs and ideas of a culture.

SET A PURPOSE **Think about** the title and genre of this text, and look at the illustrations. What lesson do you think the characters will learn? Write your ideas below.

CRITICAL VOCABULARY

tempting

quantities

ominously

Build Background:
Nigerian Folktale Origin

WHY THE SKY IS FAR AWAY

A Nigerian Folk Tale

retold by Marci Stillerman

illustrated by Salim Busuru

1   In the beginning, the sky was close to the earth, and the people didn't have to work for their food. All they had to do was cut away a piece of sky to eat. It tasted delicious, like meat or corn or honey or anything else they felt like eating. Since they didn't have to hunt for their food, all they did was weave and carve and tell stories all day.

2   When the great King Oba wanted to give a party, his servants would cut out pieces of the sky and shape them into wonderful forms—animals, diamonds, leaves, or flowers.

3   But as time went on, the people forgot to appreciate the sky. They took their food for granted, and they became wasteful. They cut far more sky than they needed and threw what they didn't use onto the garbage heap.

4   The sky became angry because of the waste and the people's ingratitude for his gift.

5   One day, the sky grew very dark. The people were frightened.

6   "Oba," a voice boomed above the king's palace. "Wasteful one, king of wasteful, ungrateful people. If you continue to waste food, you will have no more of the sky to cut."

7   Oba was terrified. He sent messengers all over his kingdom. "Take only what you need," they warned. "The sky is angry because of your greed. Stop wasting the sky, or there will be trouble."

8   For a while, the people were very careful. They cut only what they needed from the sky. They ate all they took. Nothing was thrown on the garbage heap. Nothing was wasted.

9   Once every year there was a great festival in Oba's kingdom in celebration of his greatness. All the people looked forward to wearing their best clothes, dancing all day and night, and feasting on wonderful foods.

10   Oba's servants prepared magnificent food. They pulled pieces of sky down and shaped them into flowers and animals and every imaginable form. They colored them and cooked them and placed them on huge platters so that the food looked tempting and inviting.

11   The people came in gorgeous robes. Music played, and everyone danced. Soon the people became hungry and started to eat. The food was so delicious that they ate and ate until everything was gone.

> **tempting**   If something is tempting, it's something you want very much.

12   But the people were greedy and wanted more, even though they were no longer hungry. They pulled down great quantities of the sky and gobbled them up. What they couldn't stuff into themselves, they threw on the garbage heap. Greedy and wasteful, they forgot all about the sky's warning.

13   Suddenly, while the festival was still going on, the sky grew ominously dark. Thunder rumbled and roared, and fearsome knives of lightning sliced through the sky.

14   "People of the earth," the sky boomed, "you are wasteful and greedy. I warned you. I will no longer give you food. You will have to work to eat."

quantities   Quantities are amounts that can be counted.
ominously   If something acts ominously, it makes you think that something bad might happen.

385

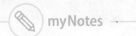

15   The sky sailed up high above the earth, far out of the reach of the tallest person. Ever since then, no one has been able to reach up and grab a piece of it, and the people must work hard on farms and in factories for their food.

Collaborative Discussion

Look back at what you wrote on page 380. With a partner discuss your ideas about the lesson the characters learn. Then work with a group to discuss the questions below. Refer to details in *Why the Sky Is Far Away* to support your ideas. Take notes for your responses.

1 Review page 382. How is the sky in the story different from the sky we see?

2 Reread pages 384–385. Why do the people forget the sky's warning during Oba's festival?

3 What can you tell about the sky from what it said and what it did?

Listening Tip

Listen closely to the ideas other speakers share. Keep those ideas in mind as you decide if you agree or disagree.

Speaking Tip

Restate a speaker's idea in your own words. Then share another example or a related idea.

Write a Lesson

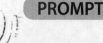

PROMPT ....

Why the Sky Is Far Away is a Nigerian folktale that tells how the sky got angry at people for being greedy and wasteful. Like most folktales, it teaches an important lesson to readers.

Imagine you are a teacher who needs to explain to students the difference between a story's topic and its theme. Write a paragraph that you could hand out to students that explains this difference. Demonstrate the difference using examples from *Why the Sky Is Far Away*.

PLAN ....

Write definitions for the terms *topic* and *theme*. Under each definition, write notes about the text that you could use to demonstrate the meaning of the word.

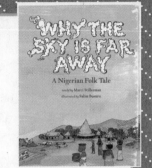

Now write your lesson that explains the difference between the terms *topic* and *theme*.

✓	Make sure your lesson
☐	defines the terms *topic* and *theme*.
☐	identifies the topic and theme of *Why the Sky Is Far Away*.
☐	is written so young students can understand it.
☐	is free of errors in capitalization, punctuation, and spelling.

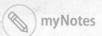
Notice & Note

Again and Again

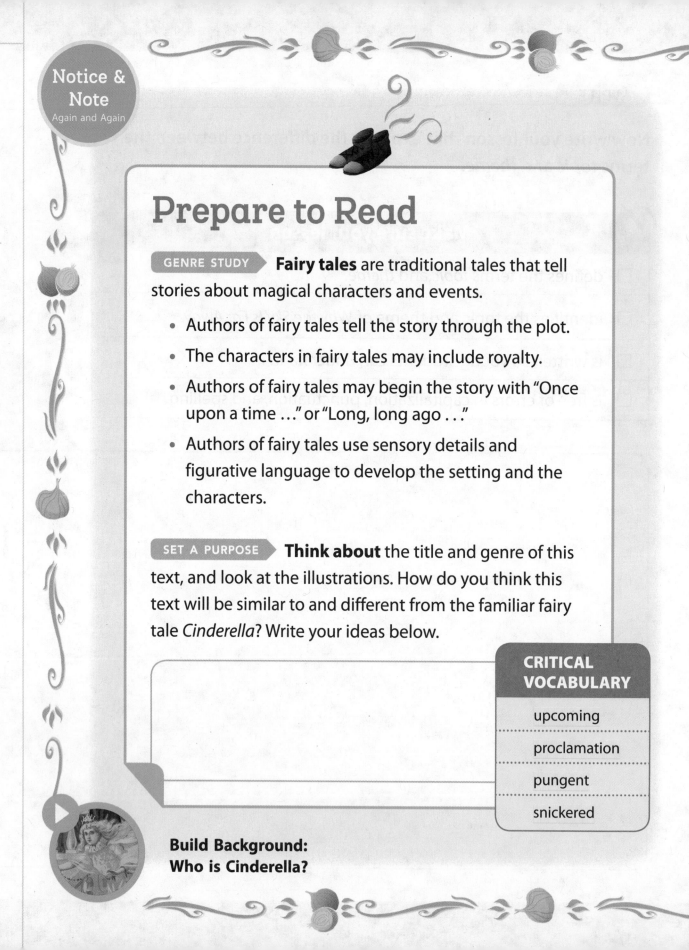

Prepare to Read

GENRE STUDY **Fairy tales** are traditional tales that tell stories about magical characters and events.

- Authors of fairy tales tell the story through the plot.

- The characters in fairy tales may include royalty.

- Authors of fairy tales may begin the story with "Once upon a time …" or "Long, long ago . . ."

- Authors of fairy tales use sensory details and figurative language to develop the setting and the characters.

SET A PURPOSE **Think about** the title and genre of this text, and look at the illustrations. How do you think this text will be similar to and different from the familiar fairy tale *Cinderella*? Write your ideas below.

CRITICAL VOCABULARY

upcoming

proclamation

pungent

snickered

Build Background: Who is Cinderella?

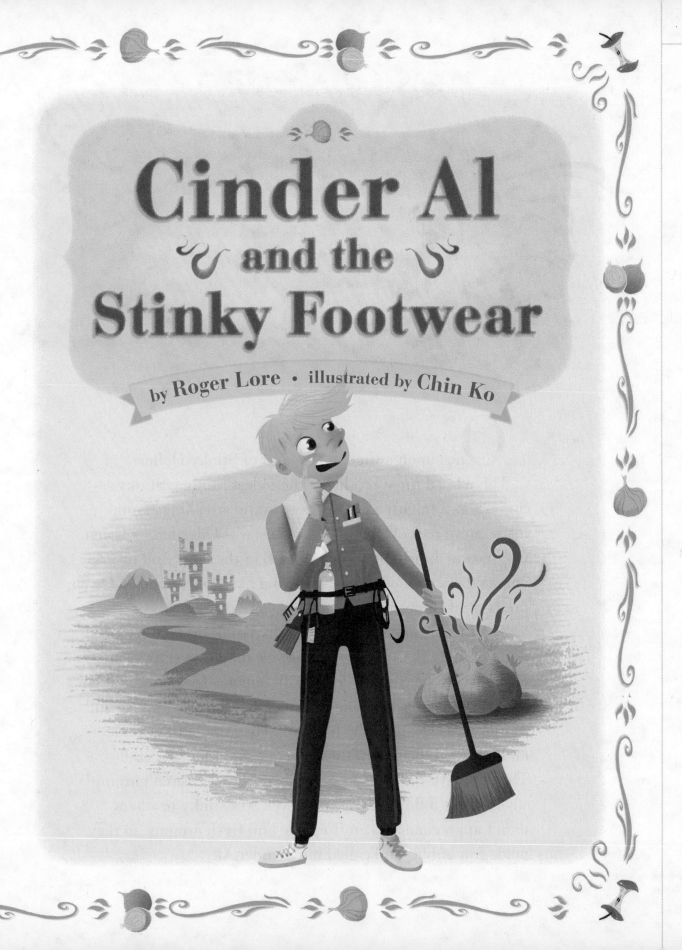

Cinder Al
and the
Stinky Footwear

by Roger Lore • illustrated by Chin Ko

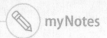

1   Once upon a time in the land of Stinky Hollow . . .

2   There lived three brothers. The oldest brother, Stinky
Steve, was a mighty skunk wrestler, and wrestling skunks
made Steve reek. The middle brother was Odoriferous Owen.
Owen owned the biggest onion farm in the land, and he grew
onions the size of ostriches! Growing giant onions made Owen
pretty stinky, too.

3   The third brother was Al. Al didn't stink. In fact, he loved
nothing more than keeping things clean and sweetly scented.
He polished the cottage floors with lemony-fresh oils, and he
used lavender-scented soap to wash his clothes. His favorite
pastime was cleaning the fireplace. He gathered the cinders
and replaced them with flower petals and scented candles.
Thanks to Al, the cottage (when his brothers weren't around)
smelled like a flower shop. However, Al's stinky brothers
didn't appreciate a clean fireplace and fresh aromas, so they
made fun of him and called him Cinder Al.

myNotes

4   Stinky Hollow was ruled by Princess Peeyu. Princess
Peeyu was an even mightier skunk wrestler than Stinky
Steve, and she could pin five skunks at one time. She was a
more fantastic farmer than Odoriferous Owen. She grew ten-
ton garlic in the Palace Garden.

5   Because of these mighty stinky abilities, Princess Peeyu
was the stinkiest person in Stinky Hollow and she had no one
to dance with at the upcoming Palace Ball, so she issued a
royal proclamation.

> **upcoming**   If an event is upcoming, it will take place soon.
> **proclamation**   A proclamation is a statement or message about an important matter that everyone needs to know.

HEAR YE, HEAR YE, BLAH BLAH, ETC., ETC.

**THE STINKY BACHELOR WHO
CAN WEAR THE STINKY FOOTWEAR WILL
GET TO DANCE WITH PRINCESS PEEYU AT
THE PALACE BALL.**

(IF IT ALL WORKS OUT, THE TWO OF YOU MIGHT
GET MARRIED . . . BUT NO PROMISES.)

6   The stinky footwear was nothing more than a pair of elegant dancing shoes. However, these shoes came with one pungent problem. They reeked. They stank. They smelled like the biggest skunk sitting in a garbage dump on the hottest day of the year and eating four rotten eggs! Wearing these shoes and surviving their terrible stench wouldn't be easy, even for the stinkiest bachelors in Stinky Hollow.

7   However . . .

8   The rotten reek of the stinky footwear didn't stop Stinky Steve. He followed his nose straight to the palace. When he placed the footwear onto his feet, his eyes watered, his stomach churned, and his nose stung! Steve couldn't stand the stench, and he raced out of the palace, screaming, "I'd rather sniff seventy skunks!"

9   Odoriferous Owen went next, and he did far worse than his smelly brother. After one whiff of the stinky footwear, Owen fainted! He passed out, right in front of Princess Peeyu!

---

pungent   If something is pungent, it has a strong smell that may be unpleasant.

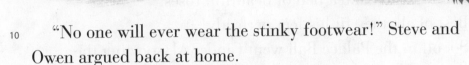

10   "No one will ever wear the stinky footwear!" Steve and Owen argued back at home.

11   "But I haven't tried yet," said Cinder Al.

12   Cinder Al's brothers snickered. "You? You'll never be able to stand that stench, Cinder Al!"

13   That night, Cinder Al had a visit from his Fragrant Fairy Godmother (who always smelled as fresh as daisies on a beautiful spring day).

> **snickered**   If someone snickered, they laughed in a rude or disrespectful way.

14   "Listen, Al. You will wear the stinky footwear and dance with Princess Peeyu. Here's what to do."

15   The next day, Cinder Al headed straight to the palace. With him, he carried a clothespin and a bag of cleaning supplies. He clipped the clothespin on his nose. Then he gave the stinky footwear the cleaning of a lifetime, and in no time, the slippers smelled like a bed of beautiful roses.

16   Best of all, they fit his feet perfectly!

17   So, off to the Palace Ball went Cinder Al, sporting the stinky footwear and a clothespin. (While Princess Peeyu was really nice, she still liked to wrestle skunks and grow garlic, which is, of course, disturbingly stinky.)

18   The princess and Al hit it off like onions and liver! (Eww, stinky!)

19   . . . and the rest?

20   Well, let's just say everything worked out happily ever after . . .

Collaborative Discussion

Look back at what you wrote on page 390. With a partner discuss your ideas about how *Cinder Al and the Stinky Footwear* is similar to and different from *Cinderella*. Then work with a group to discuss the questions below. Refer to details in *Cinder Al and the Stinky Footwear* to support your ideas. Take notes for your responses.

1 Reread page 392. How does Cinder Al get his name?

2 Reread page 393. Why are the brothers willing to try on the stinky footwear and dance with the princess?

3 What makes the stinky footwear smell even worse than Stinky Steve and Odoriferous Owen?

Listening Tip

Listen carefully when a group member asks you a question. What information is the speaker asking for?

Speaking Tip

When a group member asks you a question, first restate his or her question to make sure you understand what he or she is asking.

Write an Opinion Post

Cinder Al and the Stinky Footwear is a silly twist on the well-known fairy tale about Cinderella and the glass slipper. The author's voice is so strong in this text that you can almost hear it as you read!

Imagine that your class has an online newsletter with a section called *Just for Laughs*, and it's your turn to write this feature. Write a post about what you think makes *Cinder Al and the Stinky Footwear* so funny. Include examples and details from the story in your post. Also mention specific word choices the author makes which contribute to the humor. Don't forget to use some of the Critical Vocabulary words in your writing.

Make a list of funny words and phrases the author uses.

WRITE

Now write your opinion post about why the text is so funny.

Make sure your opinion post
☐ begins with an introduction and ends with a conclusion.
☐ clearly states your opinion.
☐ provides evidence from the text to support your opinion.
☐ uses linking words such as *because, since*, and *for example* to connect your opinion and the reasons that support it.

Prepare to Read

GENRE STUDY **Folktales** are traditional stories that have been passed down orally from one generation to another.

- Authors of folktales tell the story through the plot.
- Folktales include a moral or lesson learned.
- Folktales might include magic creatures or animals that talk as characters.
- Folktales include the beliefs and ideas of a culture.

SET A PURPOSE **Think about** the title and genre of this text, and look at the illustrations. What lesson do you think the main character will learn? Write your ideas below.

CRITICAL VOCABULARY

theft

inspected

sympathetic

suspicious

reputation

crafty

**Meet the Author:
Joe Hayes**

Compay Mono and Comay Jicotea

retold by Joe Hayes ✳ *illustrated by* Lucia Franco

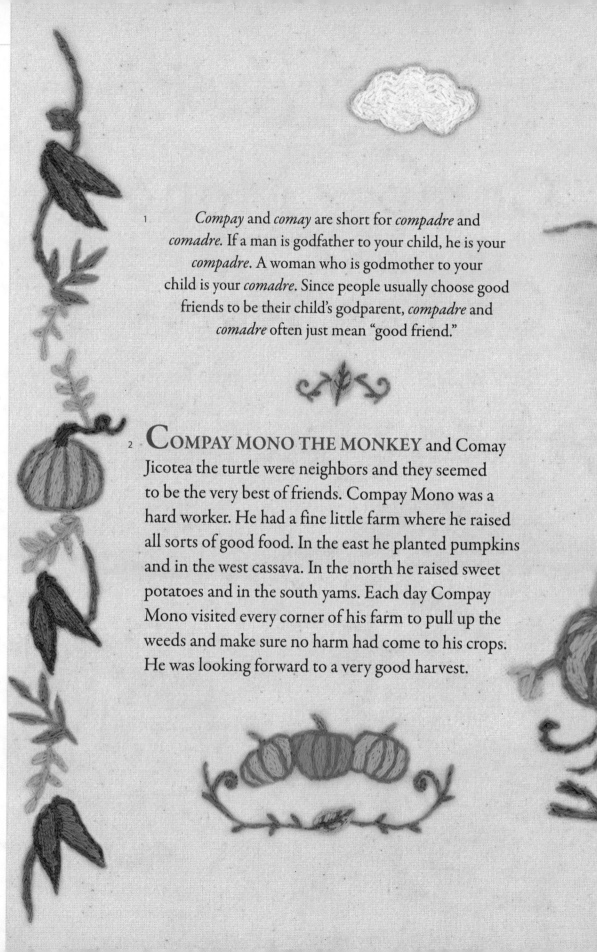

1   *Compay* and *comay* are short for *compadre* and *comadre*. If a man is godfather to your child, he is your *compadre*. A woman who is godmother to your child is your *comadre*. Since people usually choose good friends to be their child's godparent, *compadre* and *comadre* often just mean "good friend."

2   COMPAY MONO THE MONKEY and Comay Jicotea the turtle were neighbors and they seemed to be the very best of friends. Compay Mono was a hard worker. He had a fine little farm where he raised all sorts of good food. In the east he planted pumpkins and in the west cassava. In the north he raised sweet potatoes and in the south yams. Each day Compay Mono visited every corner of his farm to pull up the weeds and make sure no harm had come to his crops. He was looking forward to a very good harvest.

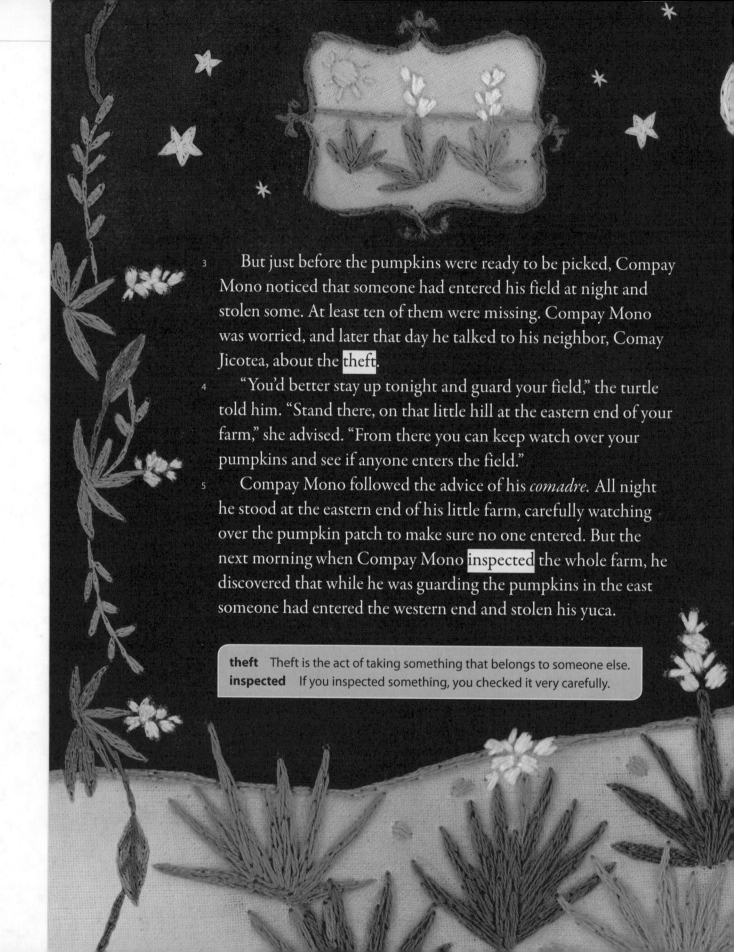

3   But just before the pumpkins were ready to be picked, Compay Mono noticed that someone had entered his field at night and stolen some. At least ten of them were missing. Compay Mono was worried, and later that day he talked to his neighbor, Comay Jicotea, about the theft.

4   "You'd better stay up tonight and guard your field," the turtle told him. "Stand there, on that little hill at the eastern end of your farm," she advised. "From there you can keep watch over your pumpkins and see if anyone enters the field."

5   Compay Mono followed the advice of his *comadre*. All night he stood at the eastern end of his little farm, carefully watching over the pumpkin patch to make sure no one entered. But the next morning when Compay Mono inspected the whole farm, he discovered that while he was guarding the pumpkins in the east someone had entered the western end and stolen his yuca.

theft   Theft is the act of taking something that belongs to someone else.
inspected   If you inspected something, you checked it very carefully.

6   Compay Mono told Comay Jicotea what had happened.

7   "You must have fallen asleep," his *comadre* told him. "Tonight let me guard your farm. The thief will probably enter the southern field this time. I'll stand guard there so that no one can steal your *ñames*."

8   Compay Mono agreed, and that night while Comay Jicotea guarded the yams in the southern field, someone stole the *boniatos* in the northern field.

9   The next day Compay Mono told the turtle what had happened. Of course, she was very surprised and sympathetic. "How could that be?" she said shaking her head. "I never closed my eyes all night long. This must be a very clever thief."

> **sympathetic**   When you are sympathetic to someone, you are kind and understanding about his or her situation.

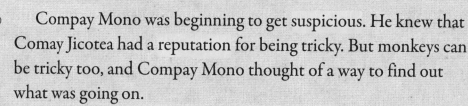

10   Compay Mono was beginning to get suspicious. He knew that Comay Jicotea had a reputation for being tricky. But monkeys can be tricky too, and Compay Mono thought of a way to find out what was going on.

11   "Yes," the monkey said to his *comadre,* "there must be a very clever and dangerous thief in these parts. The next thing you know they'll come into my house and steal my money. I know what I'd better do. I'm going to hide all my money up in the loft. No one would ever think of looking for it up there."

12   That night Compay Mono lay awake in bed listening. Late in the night he heard someone tugging at the door. Slowly it opened and then in came the humped-back form of Comay Jicotea. She headed straight toward the loft and began climbing the ladder.

13   Compay Mono jumped out of bed and grabbed her. "You're the thief!" he shouted. "You're the one who stole my pumpkins and my yams and my yuca. And you thought you'd steal all my money too. I ought to throw you into the fire!"

suspicious   If you are suspicious of someone, you are untrusting of that person.

reputation   If you have a reputation for something, others know or remember you for that thing.

14   Comay Jicotea looked very ashamed. "You're right," she said. "I deserve to be punished. But it won't help to throw me into the fire. My shell won't burn and I'll never learn a lesson from that. You should throw me into the river. I'm terrified of the cold water, but I know it's just what I deserve."

15   As everyone knows, monkeys are afraid of water, and so what that crafty Jicotea said made sense to Compay Mono. He picked up the turtle and ran to the river with her. He threw her as far out into the water as he could, and, of course, the tricky little Comay Jicotea swam away laughing to herself.

16   To this day, Comay Jicotea sometimes comes out to sun herself on the bank of the river, but she spends most of her time in the water. She knows Compay Mono still wants to catch her and punish her, but she knows that if she just jumps into the river, the monkey will never dive in after her.

crafty   Someone who is crafty uses clever or tricky ways to get what he or she wants.

Collaborative Discussion

Look back at what you wrote on page 400. With a partner discuss your ideas about the lesson the main character learns. Then work with a group to discuss the questions below. Refer to details in *Compay Mono and Comay Jicotea* to support your ideas. Take notes for your responses.

1 Reread pages 404–406. Why does Compay Mono become suspicious of his neighbor?

2 Review page 406. Why does Compay Mono tell Comay Jicotea that there is money hidden in the loft of his home?

3 In what ways are Compay Mono and Comay Jicotea alike? In what ways are they different?

Listening Tip

Look at a speaker as he or she shares ideas. The look on a speaker's face can help you understand more about his or her comments.

Speaking Tip

As you finish sharing your ideas with the group, ask if anyone has questions or wants to add to what you have said.

Write a Trickster Tale

PROMPT

In *Compay Mono and Comay Jicotea*, Mono the Monkey learns he should not trust Jicotea the Turtle. Trickster tales such as this are fun ways to learn important lessons about life.

Now write your own trickster tale. Think of it as a sequel to the story you just read. Use the same characters and setting as the text, but the plot should tell about a new conflict and resolution. Maybe this time Compay Mono is the trickster, or maybe he still has not learned his lesson. The choice is yours!

PLAN

Make a list of possible conflicts you could write about. Then list ways each conflict could be resolved.

WRITE

Now write your new trickster tale about Mono and Jicotea.

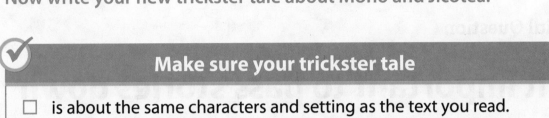

Make sure your trickster tale

- ☐ is about the same characters and setting as the text you read.

- ☐ uses words like *first*, *next*, and *then* to signal the order of events.

- ☐ includes lines of dialogue between the characters and descriptions of their feelings.

- ☐ ends with a clear resolution to the conflict.

 Essential Question

Why is it important to pass stories down to the next generation?

Write a Story

PROMPT Think about the storytellers who might have first shared the stories you read in this module.

Imagine that your school library wants to add to its collections of stories. You have been asked to write a story like one a storyteller of long ago might have told. Review the texts for ideas and examples to help you write your story.

I will write a story about _____.

 ☑	**Make sure your story**
☐	introduces the main character or narrator.
☐	explains a problem the character has.
☐	tells about events in an order that makes sense.
☐	shows what characters say and do as they react to events.
☐	has an ending that shares a lesson or message.

·· Map your ideas.

What lesson or message will your story explain? How will the characters learn that lesson? Look back at your notes and review the texts for ideas.

Use the story map below to fill in your story's setting and characters. Add notes about the lesson the characters learn and what they say and do to learn it. Use Critical Vocabulary words where you can.

My Topic: _____

Setting	Characters
Problem	
Events	
Solution/Lesson	

DRAFT .... Write your story.

Use the information you wrote on page 413 to draft your story. Tell about
the characters and the problem they have at the **beginning** of your story.

Write the events that happen in the **middle** of your story. What do the
characters say and do?

Write an **ending** that shares the lesson your characters learn.

The revision and editing steps give you a chance to look carefully at your writing and make changes. Work with a partner to determine whether you have explained your ideas clearly to readers. Use these questions to help you evaluate and improve your story.

✓ PURPOSE/ FOCUS	ORGANIZATION	EVIDENCE	LANGUAGE/ VOCABULARY	CONVENTIONS
☐ Does my story tell about a lesson the characters learn? ☐ Did I only include events important to my story?	☐ Is there a clear beginning, middle, and ending? ☐ Does the order of events make sense?	☐ Did I use examples from texts in the module? ☐ Does the story tell what characters say and do?	☐ Did I use linking words and phrases to show when events happen?	☐ Did I indent each paragraph? ☐ Did I use quotation marks correctly? ☐ Did I use pronouns correctly?

PUBLISH ·· Share your work.

Create a Finished Copy Make a final copy of your story. You may want to add illustrations to show important events. Consider these options to share your story:

1. Add your story to the class or school library for others to enjoy.

2. Read your story aloud to the class.

3. Post your story on a class or school website. Invite readers to comment or share their own stories.

Glossary

This glossary contains meanings and pronunciations for some of the words in this book. The Full Pronunciation Key shows how to pronounce each consonant and vowel in a special spelling. At the bottom of the glossary pages is a shortened form of the full key.

Full Pronunciation Key

CONSONANT SOUNDS

b	**bib**, ca**bb**age	r	**r**oar, **rh**yme
ch	**ch**ur**ch**, sti**tch**	s	mi**ss**, **s**au**c**e,
d	**d**ee**d**, mail**ed**,		**sc**ene, **s**ee
	pu**dd**le	sh	**di**sh, **sh**ip, **s**ugar,
f	**f**ast, **f**i**f**e, o**ff**,		ti**ss**ue
	phrase, rou**gh**	t	**t**igh**t**, stopp**ed**
g	**g**a**g**, **g**et, fin**g**er	th	ba**th**, **th**in
h	**h**at, **wh**o	th	ba**the**, **th**is
hw	**wh**ich, **wh**ere	v	ca**v**e, **v**al**v**e, **v**ine
j	**j**u**dg**e, **g**em	w	**w**ith, **w**olf
k	**c**at, **k**i**ck**, s**ch**ool	y	**y**es, **y**olk, on**i**on
kw	**ch**oir, **qu**ick	z	ro**s**e, si**z**e,
l	**l**id, need**le**, ta**ll**		**x**ylophone,
m	a**m**, **m**an, du**mb**		**z**ebra
n	**n**o, sudd**en**	zh	gara**g**e,
ng	thi**ng**, i**nk**		plea**s**ure, vi**s**ion
p	**p**o**p**, ha**pp**y		

VOWEL SOUNDS

ă	p**a**t, l**au**gh	ô	**a**ll, c**au**ght, f**or**,
ā	**a**pe, **ai**d, p**ay**		p**aw**
â	**air**, c**are**, w**ear**	oi	b**oy**, n**oi**se, **oi**l
ä	f**a**ther, ko**a**la,	ou	c**ow**, **ou**t
	yard	o͝o	f**u**ll, b**oo**k, w**o**lf
ĕ	p**e**t, pl**ea**sure,	o͞o	b**oo**t, r**u**de, fr**ui**t,
	any		fl**ew**
ē	b**e**, b**ee**, **ea**sy,	ŭ	c**u**t, fl**oo**d,
	pian**o**		r**ou**gh, s**o**me
ĭ	**i**f, p**i**t, b**u**sy	û	c**ir**cle, f**ur**, h**ear**d,
ī	r**i**de, b**y**, p**ie**,		t**er**m, t**ur**n, **ur**ge,
	h**igh**		w**or**d
î	d**ear**, d**eer**,	yo͝o	c**ure**
	f**ier**ce, m**ere**	yo͞o	ab**u**se, **u**se
ŏ	h**o**rrible, p**o**t	ə	**a**go, sil**e**nt,
ō	g**o**, r**ow**, t**oe**,		penc**i**l, lem**o**n,
	th**ough**		circ**u**s

STRESS MARKS

Primary Stress ´: biology [bī•**ŏl**´•ə•jē]
Secondary Stress ´: biological [bī´•ə•**lŏj**´•ĭ•kəl]

A

agriculture (ăg′•rĭ•kŭl′•chər) *n*. Agriculture is the practice of farming, producing crops, and raising animals. A tractor is used in agriculture to pull machinery that plows and plants crops.

appease (ə•pēz′) *v*. If you appease someone, you try to make the person less angry by giving in to what he or she wants. When my hungry brother starts crying, dad tries to appease him with a bottle.

arbor (är′•bər) *n*. An arbor is a shady passageway made of vines or branches. The arbor was the perfect spot to rest after playing in the hot sun.

assistant (ə•sĭs′•tənt) *n*. An assistant is someone who helps another person do his or her work. The veterinary assistant helps hold the dog in place while the vet bandages the dog's leg.

B

baffled (bă′•fəld) *adj*. If you are baffled, you are confused. Erik has a baffled expression when he sees the results of his experiment.

bared (bârd) *v*. If an animal bared its teeth, it showed them in an angry way. The dog bared his teeth to keep strangers out of the yard.

barren (băr′•ən) *adj*. If an area of land is barren, it is dry and cannot grow plants or trees. The barn is the only building in the barren field.

belched (bĕlchd) *v*. If a volcano or chimney belched, it suddenly pushed out a large amount of smoke or fire. The volcano loudly belched out smoke and fire.

blooming (blōō′•mĭng) *v*. When trees or plants are blooming, their flowers are out and open. The tree reveals the most beautiful flowers when it is blooming.

breakthrough (brāk′•thrōō′) *n*. If you make a breakthrough, you make an important discovery after many tries. Ron makes a breakthrough when he figures out how to solve the problem.

brilliant (brĭl′•yənt) *adj*. When a person, idea, or thing is brilliant, it is extremely clever or skillful. Benjamin Franklin was a brilliant genius when it came to his experiments with electricity.

burly (bûr′•lē) *adj*. Someone who is burly is big and strong. The burly blacksmith was strong enough to mold and shape the metal.

ōō b**oo**t / ou **ou**t / ŭ c**u**t / û f**u**r / hw **wh**ich / th **th**in / *th* **th**is / zh vi**si**on / ə **a**go, sil**e**nt, penc**i**l, lem**o**n, circ**u**s

C

cable (**kā'**·bəl) *n.* A cable is a bundle of wires with a thick covering that is used to carry electricity. We use a cable to connect electricity, monitors, and printers to computers.

chimed (chīmd) *v.* If you chimed in, you said something to agree with what someone else said. When Suzy said that horses are her favorite animals, Max chimed in to say that he also loves horses.

cinders (**sĭn'**·dərz) *n.* Cinders are small black pieces of ash that are left after a fire has burned. The outdoor fire pit is full of cinders.

communal (kə·**myōō'**·nəl) *adj.* Something is communal when it is shared by a group of people in the same community or area. We take care of our plot in the communal garden.

compact (kəm·**păkt'**, **kŏm'**·păkt') *adj.* Things that are compact can fit in a small space. There are many new compact cars that take up less space and use less fuel than larger cars.

concluded (kən·**klōō'**·dĭd) *v.* When you have concluded something, you have ended it. We knew the show had concluded when the lights went down and the actors took a bow.

— **Word Origins** —

concluded One meaning of *concluded* is "to end; close; finish." *Conclude* comes from the Latin prefix *con–*, which means "completely," and *claudere*, which means "*to close.*"

confesses (kən·**fĕs'**·ĕs) *v.* If someone confesses something, he or she admits to doing or saying something wrong. My little brother confesses to breaking the flowerpot.

— **Word Origins** —

confesses The word *confesses* comes from the Latin past participle *confiteri*, which means "acknowledge."

contraption (kən·**trăp'**·shən) *n.* A contraption is a mechanical gadget or device that has a certain purpose. After school, we worked together on a contraption to help our teacher pass out papers.

converted (kən·**vûr'**·tĭd) *v.* When something is converted, it is changed to a different form or changed in some important way. Wind energy can be converted to electrical energy.

ă rat / ā pay / â care / ä father / ĕ pet / ē be / ĭ pit / ī pie / î fierce / ŏ pot / ō go / ô paw, for / oi oil / ōō book /

crafty (krăf′•tē) *adj.* Someone who is crafty uses clever or tricky ways to get what he or she wants. Olivia found a crafty way to convince her mom to let her eat a strawberry before dinner.

craze (krāz) *n.* If there is a craze for something, it is very popular for a period of time. Using a spinner is a craze to help stop fidgeting.

crowded (krou′•dĭd) *v.* If you crowded a space with something, you filled it up with no room left for anything else. The people crowded around each other on the train.

cumbersome (kŭm′•bər•səm) *adj.* Something that is cumbersome is heavy and hard to carry or wear. The boxes are too cumbersome to carry.

curds (kûrdz) *n.* Curds are the lumps that form in milk when it turns sour. The bowl is filled with cottage cheese curds.

D

dairy (dâr′•ē) *n.* A dairy is a place where milk is prepared for drinking or is made into other products, like butter, cream, and cheese. The best part of our trip to the dairy was getting to pet the cows.

deposited (dĭ•pŏz′•ĭ•tĭd) *v.* If you deposited something in a place, you left it there. I deposited my coins into the piggy bank.

device (dĭ•vīs′) *n.* A device is a tool or machine that has a certain purpose. Our class tablet is a device that can be used for schoolwork.

dictation (dĭk•tā′•shən) *n.* The word *dictation* describes the act of writing down words that have been spoken. Haley takes dictation while her teacher presents the lesson.

Word Origins

dictation The word *dictation* derives from the Latin word *dictiō*, relating to the choice of words in speech and writing. Thus *dictation* is the process of dictating speech into writing.

dynamo (dī′•nə•mō′) *n.* A person who is a dynamo has a lot of energy and is very good at what she does. Ryan is a dynamo who wins often when playing chess.

ōō b**oo**t / ou **ou**t / ŭ c**u**t / û f**u**r / hw **wh**ich / th **th**in / *th* **th**is / zh vi**si**on / ə **a**go, sil**e**nt, penc**i**l, lem**o**n, circ**u**s

E

engineer (ĕn'•jə•**nîr'**) *n.* An engineer is a person who uses science to design and build machines. Kate was always building something, and we knew she would be a great engineer some day.

environmental (ĕn•vī'•rən•**mĕn'**•tl) *adj.* Something that is environmental is connected to protecting Earth's land, water, animals, and air. Many children join environmental groups to help protect the Earth.

era (îr'•ə) *n.* An era is a period of time in history. Dinosaurs lived in an era long ago.

F

factories (făk'•tə•rēz) *n.* Factories are large buildings where things are built or made by people and machines. Cars are built in factories.

fellowship (fĕl'•ō•shĭp') *n.* A fellowship is a friendly feeling between people who share experiences. A fellowship formed among the volunteers as they worked together.

flexible (flĕk'•sə•bəl) *adj.* If something is flexible, it can bend or change shape without breaking. Sammy is a great addition to our gymnastic team because she is so flexible.

flickered (flĭk'•ərd) *v.* If a flame flickered, it gave off a light that moved in an unsteady way. All of the birthday candles flickered.

folklore (fōk'•lôr') *n.* Folklore is the traditional sayings, beliefs, and stories within a community. The puppet show told a story that was part of our folklore.

forage (fôr'•ĭj) *v.* When animals forage, they search through an area to find food. Bears like to forage for berries in the forest.

G

gallant (găl'•ənt) *adj.* If you are gallant, you are thoughtful and very brave. Christina looks very gallant dressed as a superhero.

garlands (gär'•lənds) *n.* Garlands are ropes made of flowers or leaves. The chairs at the wedding were decorated with garlands.

greenhouses (grēn'•hou'•səs) *n.* Greenhouses are glass buildings that are used to grow plants and flowers. Greenhouses provide plants with the warm and safe climate that they need to survive outside of their natural environment.

ă rat / ā pay / â care / ä father / ĕ pet / ē be / ĭ pit / ī pie / î fierce / ŏ pot / ō go / ô paw, for / oi oil / o͝o book /

grove (grōv) *n.* A grove is a group of trees that are close to one another. The orchard has a grove of apple trees.

growth (grōth) *n.* Growth happens when someone or something gets older and/or bigger. The scientists measured the growth of the baby turtle.

H

hatch (hăch) *v.* An animal will hatch from an egg when it breaks out of the shell by itself. We were amazed when we saw the turtle hatch from its egg.

I

inherit (ĭn•hĕr′•ĭt) *v.* When you inherit something, it is given to you, usually by a parent or grandparent. Someday, Sheena will inherit the jewelry her grandmother leaves her.

innovative (ĭn′•ə•vā′•tĭv) *adj.* An innovative idea is one that has never been thought of before. They are building an innovative tool.

inspected (ĭn•spĕk′•tĭd) *v.* If you inspected something, you checked it very carefully. Robert inspected the spider using a magnifying glass.

invention (ĭn•vĕn′•shən) *n.* An invention is something created by a person that did not exist before. The invention of the telephone changed the way people communicate.

— Word Origins —

invention The word *invention* comes from the Latin word *invenire*, which means "discover."

invisible (ĭn•vĭz′•ə•bəl) *adj.* If something is invisible, it cannot be seen. The item holding up the girl is invisible.

K

keener (kē′•nər) *adj.* If an animal's senses are keener, they are better, sharper, and more developed. Security dogs are used in airports because they have a keener sense of smell than most humans.

kernels (kûr′•nəls) *n.* Kernels are the grains or seeds of plants such as corn or wheat. These kernels turn into popcorn when they are heated.

ōo b**oo**t / ou **ou**t / ŭ c**u**t / û f**u**r / hw **wh**ich / th **th**in / *th* **th**is / zh vi**si**on / ə **a**go, sil**e**nt, penc**i**l, lem**o**n, circ**u**s

L

lagoon (lə•**goon'**) *n.* A lagoon is an area of seawater that is separated from the ocean by rocks or sand. Clams and crabs live in the small lagoon because it provides protection.

larvae (**lär'**•vē) *n.* Insects that have just hatched and haven't yet changed to their adult form are called larvae. The yellow and black caterpillar larvae will grow up into beautiful monarch butterflies.

layout (**lā'**•out') *n.* A layout is a drawing or plan that shows where things are or will be. The teacher created a layout of her classroom.

lingers (**ling'**•gərs) *v.* When something lingers, it remains for a long time. The smell of the flower lingers in the air.

lurking (**lûr'**•kĭng) *v.* If an animal is lurking, it is hiding while it waits to catch another creature. The tigers are lurking in the bushes.

M

memorable (**mĕm'**•ər•ə•bəl) *adj.* When something is memorable, it is special enough that people want to remember it. The fireworks show was a memorable way to celebrate the occasion.

molt (mōlt) *v.* When insects or other animals molt, they lose their outer covering, such as skin or feathers. Snakes molt two to four times a year.

--- Word Origins ---

molt The word *molt* comes from the Latin word *mutare*, which means "to change."

mulch (mŭlch) *n.* If you put mulch in your garden, you put straw or wood chips around your plants to help protect them. He spread mulch around the newly planted tree.

myth (mĭth) *n.* A myth is a well-known story about fantastical events that happened in the past. We read a myth about the unicorns that once lived in the woods.

N

nostrils (**nŏs'**•trəls) *n.* Nostrils are openings in a nose that take in air for breathing or smelling. My nostrils help me take in the beautiful scent of the flower.

nursery (**nûr'**•sə•rē) *n.* A nursery is a place where babies or young children are cared for. Levi loves visiting his new baby brother in his nursery.

ă **r**a**t** / ā **p**a**y** / â **c**a**re** / ä **f**a**ther** / ĕ **p**e**t** / ē **b**e / ĭ **p**i**t** / ī **p**ie / î **fie**rce / ŏ **p**o**t** / ō **g**o / ô **p**a**w, for** / oi **oi**l / ŏŏ **b**oo**k** /

nutrition (noo·trĭsh'·ən) *n.* Nutrition is the process of eating the right kinds of foods to be healthy. I want to learn about good nutrition so that I will know which foods can keep me healthy.

nuzzled (nŭz'·əld) *v.* If one animal nuzzled another, it gently touched the animal with its nose and mouth. The mother deer nuzzled her fawn to keep it close.

O

ominously (ŏm'·ə·nəs·lē) *adv.* If something acts ominously, it makes you think that something bad might happen. The dark clouds approached ominously, and we knew a storm was coming.

original (ə·rĭj'·ə·nəl) *adj.* Something described as original is the first of its kind. That record player, built in the early 1900s, is a true original.

outreach (out·rēch') *n.* When a program or people offer to help others in need, it is called outreach. Samuel volunteers at a soup kitchen as part of his community outreach.

P

patch (păch) *n.* A patch of land is a small area where one type of plant grows. We like to visit the pumpkin patch each fall.

perplexed (pər·plĕkst') *adj.* If you are perplexed, you feel confused and worried about something. I feel perplexed about the test we will have next week.

pollution (pə·loo'·shən) *n.* Pollution is harmful or poisonous material in the air, water, and ground. Factories are a cause of pollution to our environment.

pounce (pouns) *v.* If you pounce, you jump on something suddenly and hold on to it. I saw the coyote pounce on its prey.

preparations (prĕp'·ə·rā'·shənz) *n.* The things that have to be done to get ready for an event are preparations. Decorating the room was a part of the preparations for the party.

prepping (prĕp·pĭng') *v.* If you are prepping something, you are preparing it, or getting it ready, for the next step. I help my mom make soup by prepping the vegetables.

---

oo b**oo**t / ou **ou**t / ŭ c**u**t / û f**u**r / hw **wh**ich / th **th**in / *th* **th**is / zh vi**s**ion / ə **a**go, sil**e**nt, penc**i**l, lem**o**n, circ**u**s

proclamation
(prŏk'•lə•mā'•shən) *n.* A proclamation is a statement or message about an important matter that everyone needs to know. The mayor announced a proclamation.

productive (prə•dŭk'•tĭv) *adj.* If you are productive, you are able to do a lot with the time and resources that you have. The most productive student will finish his daily tasks and more in a regular school day.

pungent (pŭn'•jənt) *adj.* If something is pungent, it has a strong smell that may be unpleasant. There is a pungent smell coming from the trash can.

Q

quantities (kwŏn'•tĭ•tēz) *n.* Quantities are amounts that can be counted. The art room has different quantities of paper, markers, paint, and paintbrushes.

quest (kwĕst) *n.* If you go on a quest, you go in search of something important to you. Our class put on a puppet show about a quest to find hidden treasure.

--- **Word Origins** ---

quest The word *quest* comes from the Latin word *quaerere,* which means "to ask or seek." *Quest* is the root word of *question,* which means "to ask or seek an answer."

R

radar (rā'•där') *n.* Radar is a way to find unseen objects by using radio signals. Radar is used to locate airplanes in flight.

reap (rēp) *v.* When you reap a crop, you cut and gather what you need from it. The farmer will reap the corn when it is ready for harvest.

recount (rĭ•kount') *v.* If you recount a story or events, you tell how something happened. One day, my mom will recount the stories she learned from her mom.

--- **Word Origins** ---

recount The word *recount* comes from the Old Northern French word *reconter,* which means "tell again." The prefix *re–* means "again" and is used in other English words such as *refill, refresh,* and *rebuild.*

ă **r**at / ā **p**ay / â **c**are / ä **f**ather / ĕ **p**et / ē **b**e / ĭ **p**it / ī **p**ie / î **fie**rce / ŏ **p**ot / ō **g**o / ô **p**aw, **fo**r / oi **oi**l / o͝o **b**ook /

recycled (rē•**sī'**•kəld) *adj.* When something is described as recycled, it has been used again or used in a different way. We carried the recycled materials to the curb.

refused (rĭ•**fyōōzd'**) *v.* If you refused something, you did not take it. Our dog refused to eat the new food we bought him.

renewable (rĭ•**nōō'**•ə•bəl) *adj.* Something that is renewable will always be available. Sunlight is a renewable resource that can be collected on rooftop solar panels.

reputation (rĕp'•yə•**tā'**•shən) *n.* If you have a reputation for something, others know or remember you for that thing. Ms. Tam has a reputation of being the nicest teacher at school.

residents (**rĕz'**•ĭ•dənts) *n.* Residents of a house, city, or country are the people that live there. The Garcias are the residents of a home in the Bedford community.

resources (rē'•**sôr'**•səz) *n.* The materials or things that people can use to get a job done are resources. I had all of the resources I needed to start my school project.

rotation (rō•**tā'**•shən) *n.* If things are in rotation, they take turns doing a job or serving a purpose. The coach sets up the rotation of the batting order before each game.

S

scarce (skârs) *adj.* If something is scarce, there is very little of it. Water is scarce in the riverbed.

scarlet (**skär'**•lĭt) *adj.* If something is scarlet, it is a bright red color. The roses were a deep scarlet color.

shrivel (**shrĭv'**•əl) *v.* When things shrivel, they dry out and get smaller and wrinkled. The flowers we bought for mom began to shrivel.

singles (**sĭng'**•gəls) *n.* Music singles are recordings of one song. We are practicing one of our singles before we go to the recording studio.

siphon (**sī'**•fən) *n.* A siphon is a tube or hose that is used to pull liquid in or out. The siphon is located below the eyes on the octopus.

slender (**slĕn'**•dər) *adj.* If something is slender, it is thin. The giraffe's long, slender neck allows it to reach leaves at the top of the tree.

ōō b**oo**t / ou **ou**t / ŭ c**u**t / û f**u**r / hw **wh**ich / th **th**in / *th* **th**is / zh vi**s**ion / ə **a**go, sil**e**nt, penc**i**l, lem**o**n, circ**u**s

snickered (**snĭk'**•ərd) *v.* If someone snickered, they laughed in a rude or disrespectful way. Alan snickered when his brother played with his food.

span (spăn) *n.* A span is a period of time between two events or dates, usually marking something important. Bulldogs have a life span of about 8 to 10 years.

stalk (stôk) *n.* A stalk is the main stem of a plant. The stalk of the bamboo tree extends high into the air.

storage (**stôr'**•ĭj) *n.* When something is in storage, it is put away so it can be used later. We use the attic as storage for items we do not use very often.

suspicious (sə•**spĭsh'**•əs) *adj.* If you are suspicious of someone, you are untrusting of that person. Emma is suspicious as Jake waits near her locker.

sympathetic (sĭm'•pə•**thĕt'**•ĭk) *adj.* When you are sympathetic to someone, you are kind and understanding about his or her situation. The coach offers sympathetic words to Annalisa when she is hurt.

system (**sĭs'**•təm) *n.* A system is a set of things or ideas that work together to get something done. The computer system in our school is helpful for completing electronic assignments. v

T

technology (tĕk•**nŏl'**•ə•jē) *n.* Technology is the use of science to invent useful things or to solve problems. We use technology to complete our lessons online in our classroom.

--- **Word Origins** ---

technology The word *technology* comes from the Greek word *tekhnē*, meaning "skill," and the suffix –*logy*, meaning "science or study." Other words that relate to the study of science and contain the suffix –*logy* are *biology*, *sociology*, and *geology*.

ă rat / ā pay / â care / ä father / ĕ pet / ē be / ĭ pit / ī pie / î fierce / ŏ pot / ō go / ô paw, for / oi oil / o͝o book /

tempting (tĕmp′•tĭng) *adj.* If something is tempting, it's something you want very much. The cupcakes looked so tempting as he walked by the pastry shop window!

theft (thĕft) *n.* Theft is the act of taking something that belongs to someone else. The dog was guilty of theft.

tilling (tĭl•**lĭng′**) *v.* If you are tilling the land, you are preparing the soil for farming and raising crops. The farmer is tilling the land by turning over the dirt and getting it ready for planting the seeds.

tingly (tĭng′•lē) *adj.* Something that feels tingly stings a little or feels prickly. His knee feels tingly as the nurse cleans his injury.

transplanted (trăns•**plăn′**•tĭd) *v.* If you transplanted something, you took it from the place it was growing and planted it in a new place. We transplanted the pine tree in the community park.

trumpet (**trŭm′**•pĭt) *v.* If you trumpet a message, you say it loudly and forcefully. The girl is excited to trumpet her cheer in the megaphone.

U

universal (yōō•nə•**vûr′**•səl) *adj.* When something is universal, it applies to everyone. All living things have a universal need for water.

unsuspecting (ŭn′•sə•**spĕk′**•tĭng) *adj.* If you are unsuspecting, you do not notice something that is happening or may happen. The unsuspecting antelopes did not notice the lion behind them.

upcoming (**ŭp′**•kŭm′•ĭng) *adj.* If an event is upcoming, it will take place soon. The upcoming recital will take place on the 15th of the month.

V

valuable (**văl′**•yōō•ə•bəl) *adj.* If something is valuable, it is useful, helpful, or important. The light bulb is one of the most valuable inventions.

vats (văts) *n.* Vats are large tanks or tubs that can hold water or other liquids. One of the vats was full of milk.

vertical (**vûr′**•tĭ•kəl) *adj.* Something that is vertical stands tall or points up. The arrow was vertical, pointing upward rather than sideways.

ōō b**oo**t / ou **ou**t / ŭ c**u**t / û f**u**r / hw **wh**ich / th **th**in / *th* **th**is / zh vi**s**ion / ə **a**go, sil**e**nt, penc**i**l, lem**o**n, circ**u**s

vine (vīn) *n.* A vine is a long, thin stem of a plant that grows along the ground or up and around something. The walls of the school were covered in the same type of vine.

visionary (vĭzh′•ə•nĕr′•ē) *n.* A visionary is a person who has new or unusual ideas about life in the future. Carla is a visionary because she is always imagining a way to make things better.

W

whirled (wûrld) *v.* Something that whirled turned around several times. The toy windmills whirled when air was blown on them.

willing (wĭl′•ĭng) *adj.* If you are willing to do something, you are ready to do it. Jenny had never skated, but she was willing to give it a try.

ă r**a**t / ā p**a**y / â c**a**re / ä f**a**ther / ĕ p**e**t / ē b**e** / ĭ p**i**t / ī p**ie** / î f**ie**rce / ŏ p**o**t / ō g**o** / ô p**a**w, f**or** / oi **oi**l / o͝o b**oo**k /

Index of Titles and Authors

Index of Titles and Authors

Acknowledgments

"A Bumpy Ride" by Sharon Katz Cooper and Rachel Young, illustrated by Ariane Elsammak, from *Ask* Magazine, July/August 2017. Text copyright © 2017 by Carus Publishing Company. Art copyright © 2005 by Ariane Elsammak. Reprinted by permission of Cricket Media. All Cricket Media material is copyrighted by Carus Publishing d/b/a Cricket Media, and/or various authors and illustrators. Any commercial use or distribution of material without permission is strictly prohibited. Please visit http://www.cricketmedia.com/info/licensing2 for licensing and http://www.cricketmedia.com for subscriptions.

"Compay Mono and Comay Jicotea" from *Dance, Nana, Dance: Cuban Folktales in English and Spanish* by Joe Hayes. Illustrated by Mauricio Trenard Sayago. Text copyright © 2008 by Joe Hayes. Illustrations copyright © 2008 by Mauricio Trenard Sayago. Reprinted by permission of Cinco Puntos Press.

Excerpt from *A Corner of the Universe* by Ann M. Martin. Text copyright © 2002 by Ann M. Martin. Reprinted by permission of Scholastic, Inc.

Energy Island by Allan Drummond. Copyright © 2011 by Allan Drummond. Reprinted by permission of Farrar, Straus Giroux Books for Young Readers.

Web/Electronic Versions: *Energy Island* by Allan Drummond. Copyright © 2011 by Allan Drummond. Reprinted by permission of Farrar, Straus Giroux Books for Young Readers. CAUTION: Users are warned that this work is protected under copyright laws and downloading is strictly prohibited. The right to reproduce or transfer the work via any medium must be secured with Farrar, Straus and Giroux.

Farmer Will Allen and the Growing Table by Jacqueline Briggs Martin, illustrated by Eric-Shabazz Larkin. Text copyright © 2013 by Jacqueline Briggs Martin. Illustrations copyright © 2013 by Eric-Shabazz Larkin. Reprinted by permission of Readers to Eaters.

Excerpt from *How Did that Get in My Lunchbox?* by Chris Butterworth, illustrated by Lucia Gaggiotti. Text copyright © 2011 by Chris Butterworth. Illustrations copyright © 2011 by Lucia Gaggiotti. Reprinted by permission of the publisher, Candlewick Press, on behalf of Walker Books, London.

Excerpt from *How Do You Raise a Raisin?* by Pam Muñoz Ryan, illustrated by Craig Brown. Text copyright © 2003 by Pam Muñoz Ryan. Illustrations copyright © 2003 by Craig Brown. Reprinted by permission of Charlesbridge Publishing, Inc.

Excerpt from *It's Our Garden* by George Ancona. Copyright © 2013 by George Ancona. Reprinted by permission of the publisher, Candlewick Press.

Excerpt from *Niagara Food: A Flavorful History of the Peninsula's Bounty* by Tiffany Mayer. Text copyright © 2014 by Tiffany Mayer. Reprinted by permission of Arcadia Publishing, Inc.

"The Nose Awards" from *CLICK Magazine*, February 2013. Text copyright © 2013 by Carus Publishing Company. Reprinted by permission of Cricket Media. All Cricket Media material is copyrighted by Carus Publishing d/b/a Cricket Media, and/or various authors and illustrators. Any commercial use or distribution of material without permission is strictly prohibited. Please visit http://www.cricketmedia.com/info/licensing2 for licensing and http://www.cricketmedia.com for subscriptions.

Octopus Escapes Again by Laurie Ellen Angus. Copyright © 2016 by Laurie Ellen Angus. Reprinted by permission of Dawn Publications.

One Plastic Bag: Isatou Ceesay and the Recycling Women of the Gambia by Miranda Paul, illustrated by Elizabeth Zunon. Text copyright © 2015 by Miranda Paul. Illustration copyright © 2012 by Elizabeth Zunon. reprinted by permission of Millbrook Press, a division of Lerner Publishing Group, Inc.

Rosie Revere, Engineer by Andrea Beaty, illustrated by David Roberts. Text copyright © 2013 by Andrea Beaty. Illustrations copyright © 2013 by David Roberts. Reprinted by permission of Express Permissions on behalf of Abrams Books for Young Readers, in imprint of Harry N. Abrams, Inc.

The Storyteller's Candle by Lucía González, illustrated by Lulu Delacre. Text copyright © 2008 by Lucía González. Illustrations copyright © 2008 by Lulu Delacre. Reprinted by permission of Children's Book Press, an imprint of Lee & Low Books Inc.

This Is Your Life Cycle by Heather Lynn Miller, illustrated by Michael Chesworth. Text copyright © 2008 by Heather Lynn Miller. Illustrations copyright © 2008 by Michael Chesworth. Reprinted by permission of Houghton Mifflin Harcourt Publishing Company.

Timeless Thomas by Gene Barretta. Copyright © 2012 by Gene Barretta. Reprinted by permission of Henry Holt Books for Young Readers.

Web/Electronic Versions: *Timeless Thomas* by Gene Barretta. Copyright © 2012 by Gene Barretta. Reprinted by permission of Henry Holt Books for Young Readers. CAUTION: Users are warned that this work is protected under copyright laws and downloading is strictly prohibited. The right to reproduce or transfer the work via any medium must be secured with Henry Holt and Company.

T. J. the Siberian Tiger Cub (retitled from *Tiger Math: Learning to Graph from a Baby Tiger*) by Ann Whitehead Nagda and Cindy Bickel. Text copyright © 2000 by Ann Whitehead Nagda. Reprinted by permission of Henry Holt Books for Young Readers and Ann Whitehead Nagda.

Web/Electronic Versions: *T. J. the Siberian Tiger Cub* (retitled from *Tiger Math: Learning to Graph from a Baby Tiger*) by Ann Whitehead Nagda and Cindy Bickel. Text copyright © 2000 by Ann Whitehead Nagda. Reprinted by permission of Henry Holt Books for Young Readers and Ann Whitehead Nagda. CAUTION: Users are warned that this work is protected under copyright laws and downloading is strictly prohibited. The right to reproduce or transfer the work via any medium must be secured with Henry Holt and Company.

When the Giant Stirred by Celia Godkin. Copyright © 2002 by Celia Godkin. Reprinted by permission of Fitzhenry & Whiteside, Markham, Ontario, Canada.

"Why the Sky Is Far Away" retold by Marci Stillerman, illustrated by Barbara Paxson from *Spider* Magazine, September 2007. Text copyright © 2007 by Carus Publishing Company. Reprinted by permission of Cricket Media. All Cricket Media material is copyrighted by Carus Publishing d/b/a Cricket Media, and/or various authors and illustrators. Any commercial use or distribution of material without permission is strictly prohibited. Please visit http://www.cricketmedia.com/info/licensing2 for licensing and http://www.cricketmedia.com for subscriptions.

Credits

5 (bc) ©Villiers Steyn/Shutterstock; 5 (t) ©George Grall/National Geographic/Getty Images, ©Steve Byland/Shutterstock, ©Photo Researchers/Science Source/Getty Images, ©Christopher Price/Alamy, ©marefoto/iStock /Getty Images Plus/Getty Images, ©MarkMirror/istock /Getty Images; 5 (b) ©Cindy Bickel; 7 (b) ©Hemera Technologies/Getty Images; 7 (t) ©Davies and Starr/Getty Images, ©Fuse/Corbis/Getty Images, ©Keystone-France/Gamma-Keystone/Getty Images, ©AnthonyRosenberg/iStock/Getty Images Plus/Getty Images, ©fstop123/E+/Getty Images, ©Bettmann/Getty Images, ©Chris Willson/Alamy, ©Future Publishing/Getty Images; 7 (c) ©Ariane Eisammak/Cricket Media; 8 (b) ©Snaprender/Shutterstock; 10 ©David Merron Photography/Moment/Getty Images; 12 ©imageBROKER/Alamy; 16 (b) ©George Grall/National Geographic/Getty Images; 16 (t) ©Christopher Price/Alamy; 17 (bl) ©Steve Byland/Shutterstock; 17 (cl) ©Photo Researchers/Science Source/Getty Images; 17 (tl) ©marefoto/iStock /Getty Images Plus/Getty Images;